THIS BOOK
BELONGS TO

....

....

Copyright @2023

All rights reserved. No part of this publication may be reproduced, stored in a retrieval system, or transmitted in any form or by any means, electronic, mechanical, photocopying, recording or otherwise, without the prior written permission of the Publisher.

Author's Afterthoughts

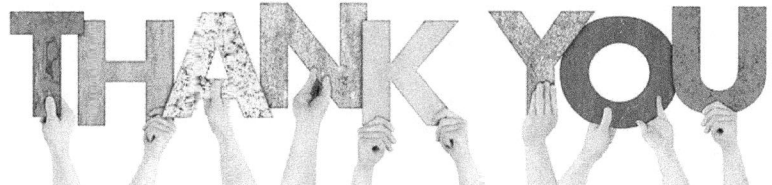

With so many books out there to choose from, I want to thank you for choosing this one and taking precious time out of your life to buy and read my work. Readers like you are the reason I take such passion in creating these books.

It is with gratitude and humility that I express how honored I am to become a part of your life and I hope that you take the same pleasure in reading this book as I did in writing it.

Can I ask one small favour? I ask that you write an honest and open review on Amazon of what you thought of the book. This will help other readers make an informed choice on whether to buy this book.

My sincerest thanks.

Table of Contents

Introduction	24
How to Draw a Goblin	25
How to Draw a Green Frog	47
How to Draw a Green Frog	65

SUMMARY

The fascination with monsters in art is a captivating and enduring subject that has intrigued artists and audiences alike throughout history. From ancient civilizations to contemporary art, monsters have been depicted in various forms, serving as a reflection of societal fears, cultural beliefs, and the human imagination.

One of the earliest examples of monster depictions can be found in ancient mythology and folklore. These mythical creatures, such as the Greek Chimera or the Egyptian Ammit, were often portrayed as hybrid beings with a combination of human and animal features. They represented the unknown and the supernatural, embodying the fears and uncertainties of ancient societies. These monsters were not only depicted in visual art but also played significant roles in literature and oral traditions, further perpetuating their fascination.

During the Renaissance period, monsters took on a new significance in art. Artists like Hieronymus Bosch and Pieter Bruegel the Elder created intricate and fantastical paintings that depicted grotesque and nightmarish creatures. These monstrous beings were often used as allegorical symbols, representing vices, sins, and the darker aspects of human nature. The fascination with monsters during this time can be seen as a reflection of the societal anxieties and moral dilemmas of the era.

In the 19th and 20th centuries, monsters continued to captivate artists, but their portrayal evolved alongside the changing cultural and technological landscape. With the rise of industrialization and scientific advancements, monsters began to take on a more scientific and psychological interpretation. Artists like H.R. Giger and Salvador Dali explored the concept of the monstrous as a manifestation of the subconscious mind, delving into the realms of surrealism and psychoanalysis.

In contemporary art, the fascination with monsters remains prevalent, albeit in a more diverse and multidimensional manner. Artists today often use monsters as a means of exploring identity, otherness, and the complexities of the human condition. They challenge societal norms and question the boundaries between the monstrous and the human. Additionally, the advent of digital art and technology has allowed for even more imaginative and realistic depictions of monsters, further fueling the fascination and intrigue surrounding them.

Overall, the fascination with monsters in art is a testament to the enduring power of the unknown and the human desire to explore and confront our deepest fears and desires. Whether they are depicted as mythical creatures, allegorical symbols, or manifestations of the subconscious, monsters continue to captivate and provoke thought, making them an integral part of artistic expression throughout history.

Understanding the fundamentals of creature design is essential for creating unique and believable creatures in various forms of media, such as movies, video games, and literature. Creature design involves the conceptualization and visualization of fictional creatures, ranging from mythical beasts to extraterrestrial beings.

One of the key aspects of creature design is anatomy. It is crucial to have a solid understanding of real-world anatomy, as it provides a foundation for creating believable creatures. By studying the skeletal structure, musculature, and proportions of real animals, designers can create creatures that adhere to the principles of biology and physics. This knowledge allows for the creation of creatures that move and behave in a realistic manner, enhancing the overall immersion and believability of the fictional world.

Another important consideration in creature design is the environment in which the creature exists. The habitat and ecological niche of a creature greatly influence its physical characteristics and adaptations. For example, a creature living in a desert environment may have evolved to have a streamlined body shape and the ability to store water, while a creature in a deep-sea environment may have bioluminescent features and a hydrodynamic body structure. Understanding these environmental factors helps designers create creatures that are well-suited to their fictional habitats.

Furthermore, the cultural and narrative context of a creature is crucial in its design. Creatures can be influenced by mythology, folklore, and cultural beliefs, which adds depth and richness to their design. For instance, a creature inspired by ancient Egyptian mythology may have hieroglyphic-like patterns on its skin or be associated with specific symbols and rituals. Additionally, the narrative purpose of a creature, whether it is a protagonist, antagonist, or a supporting character, influences its design elements such as color palette, body language, and facial expressions.

In addition to these considerations, creativity and imagination play a significant role in creature design. Designers have the freedom to push the boundaries of reality and create creatures that are truly unique and fantastical. This involves combining different elements from various sources of inspiration, such as animals, plants, and even inanimate objects, to create something entirely new. By experimenting with different shapes, textures, and color combinations, designers can bring their imaginative visions to life.

Overall, understanding the fundamentals of creature design is a multidisciplinary endeavor that combines knowledge of anatomy, environmental adaptation, cultural context, and creative thinking. By mastering these fundamentals, designers can create creatures that captivate audiences and contribute to the immersive and imaginative worlds of various forms of media.

Monsters, whether they are depicted in folklore, mythology, literature, or popular culture, often share common features that contribute to their terrifying and otherworldly nature. These features, which have been ingrained in our collective imagination, serve to evoke fear, fascination, and a sense of the unknown. While the specific characteristics of monsters may vary across different cultures and time periods, there are several recurring elements that can be identified as common features found in these creatures.

One of the most prevalent features of monsters is their physical appearance. Monsters are often depicted as grotesque, deformed, or hybrid beings, combining elements from various animals or even inanimate objects. They may possess multiple heads, limbs, or eyes, which not only adds to their intimidating presence but also symbolizes their supernatural or unnatural origins. Additionally, monsters are frequently portrayed as having exaggerated proportions, such as oversized jaws, claws, or teeth, further emphasizing their predatory nature and potential danger.

Another common feature found in monsters is their ability to instill fear through their supernatural powers or abilities. These creatures often possess extraordinary strength, speed, or agility, surpassing that of any ordinary human. They may also possess the power of flight, shape-shifting, or the ability to control elements such as fire or water. These supernatural abilities not only make monsters formidable adversaries but also contribute to their mystique and the sense of awe they inspire.

Monsters are also frequently associated with darkness, both literally and metaphorically. They are often depicted as dwelling in remote, desolate, or forbidden places, such as deep forests, caves, or haunted houses. This association with darkness and the unknown adds to their enigmatic nature and heightens the sense of danger and uncertainty they evoke. Furthermore, monsters are often portrayed as nocturnal creatures, emerging from the shadows under the cover of night, which further reinforces their association with darkness and the fear of the unknown.

In addition to their physical appearance and supernatural abilities, monsters often possess a psychological element that contributes to their terrifying nature. They are often depicted as embodying our deepest fears and anxieties, reflecting the darker aspects of human nature. For example, monsters may symbolize our fear of the unknown, our repressed desires, or our deepest insecurities. By personifying these fears, monsters become a tangible representation of our inner demons, making them all the more terrifying.

Lastly, monsters are often characterized by their relentless pursuit of their prey or victims.

Developing your unique monster concept requires a combination of creativity, imagination, and attention to detail. It is important to create a monster that stands out from the rest and captures the interest and imagination of your audience.

To begin, think about the purpose and role of your monster. Is it a villain that terrorizes a town or a hero that protects the innocent? Understanding the purpose of your monster will help you shape its characteristics and abilities.

Next, consider the physical appearance of your monster. What does it look like? Is it large and intimidating or small and cunning? Does it have multiple limbs or unique features? Think about how the physical attributes of your monster align with its purpose and role.

Once you have a general idea of the physical appearance, delve into the details. Consider the texture of its skin, the color of its eyes, and the shape of its teeth. These small details can add depth and realism to your monster concept.

Furthermore, think about the monster's abilities and powers. Does it have super strength, the ability to fly, or the power to control fire? These abilities should align with the purpose and role of your monster. Additionally, consider any weaknesses or vulnerabilities your monster may have. Every great monster needs a weakness that can be exploited by its adversaries.

In addition to the physical attributes and abilities, think about the backstory of your monster. What is its origin? How did it come to be? Understanding the backstory of your monster can add depth and complexity to its character.

Lastly, consider the environment in which your monster exists. Does it dwell in a dark cave, a haunted forest, or a bustling city? The environment can greatly influence the behavior and characteristics of your monster.

Developing a unique monster concept requires careful thought and consideration. By focusing on the purpose, physical appearance, abilities, backstory, and environment of your monster, you can create a concept that is truly one-of-a-kind. So let your imagination run wild and create a monster that will captivate and terrify your audience.

To create a visually captivating and unique alien creature, one must delve into the depths of imagination and explore the vast possibilities that lie beyond the boundaries of our known world. This task requires a careful combination of creativity, attention to detail, and an understanding of the fundamental principles of design.

First and foremost, the process of drawing an alien creature begins with envisioning its overall appearance and characteristics. Will it be humanoid or possess a completely different anatomical structure? Will it have multiple limbs, wings, or perhaps even tentacles? These initial decisions will lay the foundation for the creature's physical form.

Next, it is crucial to consider the creature's environment and habitat. Is it adapted to survive in a harsh, barren landscape or a lush, tropical paradise? This consideration will influence the creature's physical attributes, such as its skin texture, coloration, and any specialized adaptations it may possess, such as gills for underwater breathing or thick fur for insulation in extreme temperatures.

Furthermore, attention to detail is key when drawing an alien creature. Each aspect, from its facial features to its appendages, should be carefully crafted to reflect its unique nature. Consider the shape and size of its eyes, the structure of its mouth, and the arrangement of its limbs. These details will contribute to the overall believability and visual appeal of the creature.

Additionally, incorporating elements of contrast and balance can enhance the visual impact of the alien creature. Contrast can be achieved through the use of complementary colors or by juxtaposing different textures and patterns. Balance, on the other hand, ensures that the various elements of the creature's design are harmoniously arranged, creating a sense of visual equilibrium.

Moreover, exploring the concept of symbolism can add depth and meaning to the alien creature's design. Consider incorporating symbols or motifs that represent certain ideas or themes. For example, if the creature is meant to symbolize strength and resilience, incorporating elements such as sharp, angular shapes or a robust physique can help convey this message.

Lastly, the use of shading and lighting techniques can bring the alien creature to life on the page. By carefully considering the direction and intensity of light sources, one can create depth and dimension, making the creature appear more three-dimensional and realistic. Shadows can be used strategically to emphasize certain features or create a sense of mystery and intrigue.

In conclusion, drawing an alien creature is a task that requires a combination of imagination, attention to detail, and an understanding of design principles.

Designing a space monster involves a complex and creative process that requires careful consideration of various elements. The goal is to create a visually striking and unique creature that embodies the essence of a fearsome and otherworldly being. This task requires a combination of imagination, artistic skills, and an understanding of the science fiction genre.

To begin with, the designer must envision the overall appearance and characteristics of the space monster. This involves brainstorming ideas and exploring different concepts. The designer may draw inspiration from various sources such as mythology, nature, or existing fictional creatures. They must consider the monster's size, shape, and physical features, as well as its abilities and behavior.

Next, the designer must focus on the monster's anatomy and physiology. They need to determine how the creature's body is structured and how it functions. This includes deciding on the number and arrangement of limbs, the presence of wings or other appendages, and the overall body proportions. The designer must also consider the monster's internal organs, skeletal structure, and any unique adaptations it may possess.

In addition to the physical aspects, the designer must also consider the monster's visual aesthetics. This involves choosing a color palette, texture, and pattern that best represent the creature's nature. The designer may experiment with different combinations to create a visually appealing and memorable design. They must also consider how the monster's appearance may change in different environments or lighting conditions.

Furthermore, the designer must think about the monster's behavior and movement. They need to consider how the creature interacts with its environment and other beings. This includes determining its locomotion style, whether it walks, crawls, flies, or has any other unique mode of transportation. The designer must also consider the monster's behavior patterns, such as its hunting techniques, communication methods, and social structure.

Lastly, the designer must ensure that the space monster's design aligns with the intended narrative or purpose. Whether it is meant to be a terrifying antagonist in a science fiction film or a fascinating creature in a video game, the design must evoke the desired emotions and captivate the audience. The designer may need to make adjustments and revisions to the design based on feedback and the specific requirements of the project.

In conclusion, designing a space monster is a complex and intricate process that requires a combination of creativity, scientific understanding, and attention to detail. The designer must consider various aspects such as the monster's appearance, anatomy, behavior, and purpose.

To draw a haunted ghost, start by sketching a rough outline of the ghost's body. Begin with a circular shape for the head, and then draw a slightly elongated oval shape beneath it for the body. Next, add two small circles for the eyes, positioning them towards the top of the head. These eyes should have a slightly sinister and hollow look to them.

Moving on to the facial features, draw a small, curved line for the ghost's mouth, giving it a slightly open and eerie expression. Add a few jagged lines around the mouth to create the illusion of a ghostly, tattered appearance. To enhance the ghost's haunting aura, you can also draw some faint, wispy lines around the head and body, indicating a sense of movement or ethereal energy.

Now, it's time to add some details to the ghost's body. Start by drawing two elongated, curved lines extending from the bottom of the body, creating the impression of flowing, ghostly robes. These lines should be uneven and jagged, giving the ghost a more ethereal and unsettling appearance. You can also add some additional tattered edges to the robes by drawing small, irregular shapes along the bottom.

To complete the haunted ghost drawing, add some final touches. Consider adding some shading to the ghost's body and robes, using light strokes to create a sense of depth and dimension. You can also experiment with different shading techniques, such as cross-hatching or stippling, to add texture and enhance the ghostly effect.

Additionally, you can add some eerie details to the background to further enhance the haunted atmosphere. For example, you could draw a spooky graveyard scene with tombstones and a full moon in the sky. This will help set the mood and make the ghost appear even more haunting.

Remember, drawing a haunted ghost allows for creativity and personal interpretation. Feel free to experiment with different shapes, sizes, and details to create a ghost that truly captures the essence of haunting and spookiness.

The output of this request would be a comprehensive and detailed set of step-by-step coloring tutorials specifically designed for selected monsters. These tutorials would provide a thorough and easy-to-follow guide on how to color various monster illustrations, ensuring that even beginners can achieve impressive results.

Each tutorial would begin with an introduction to the monster being colored, providing information about its characteristics, backstory, and any unique features that may require special attention during the coloring process. This introduction would help the artist understand the essence of the monster and enable them to bring it to life through their coloring techniques.

Following the introduction, the tutorial would proceed with a detailed breakdown of the coloring process, starting with the basic outline of the monster. The artist would be guided through the selection of appropriate colors, considering factors such as the monster's environment, mood, and overall aesthetic. Suggestions for color combinations and shading techniques would be provided, ensuring that the artist can achieve depth and dimension in their coloring.

The tutorial would then move on to specific areas of the monster, such as its face, body, or limbs, providing step-by-step instructions on how to color each section. Techniques for creating texture, highlights, and shadows would be explained in detail, allowing the artist to add realistic and captivating details to their artwork.

Throughout the tutorial, helpful tips and tricks would be shared to enhance the artist's understanding of coloring techniques and to encourage experimentation and creativity. These tips may include suggestions for blending colors, creating gradients, or adding special effects to make the monster truly stand out.

To further assist the artist, the tutorial would also include visual aids, such as reference images or color swatches, to provide a clear visual representation of the desired outcome. This visual guidance would help the artist compare their progress and make adjustments as needed, ensuring that they stay on track and achieve the desired result.

In addition to the step-by-step instructions, the tutorial would conclude with a summary and review of the coloring process, highlighting key points and techniques covered. This summary would serve as a handy reference for the artist to revisit whenever they need a quick reminder or want to recreate the coloring process for a different monster.

Overall, the output of this request would be a comprehensive and detailed set of step-by-step coloring tutorials that cater specifically to monsters. These tutorials would empower artists of all skill levels to confidently approach the coloring process, enabling them to bring these fantastical creatures to life with their own unique artistic flair.

Building a portfolio of monster drawings involves creating a collection of artwork that showcases various imaginative and unique creatures. This process requires careful planning, creativity, and skillful execution to ensure that each monster drawing stands out and captivates the viewer.

To begin, it is essential to brainstorm and conceptualize different monster ideas. This can be done by exploring various sources of inspiration such as mythology, folklore, movies, and literature. Researching different monster archetypes and characteristics can help in developing a diverse range of creatures for the portfolio.

Once the initial ideas are formed, it is important to sketch out rough drafts of each monster. This allows for experimentation and exploration of different shapes, sizes, and features. It is during this stage that the artist can refine their ideas and make adjustments to ensure that each monster is visually appealing and unique.

After the rough drafts are complete, the artist can move on to creating more detailed and refined drawings. This involves paying attention to the finer details such as textures, shading, and proportions. The use of different artistic techniques and mediums, such as pencil, ink, or digital tools, can further enhance the visual impact of the monster drawings.

In addition to the technical aspects, it is crucial to consider the narrative and storytelling elements of each monster. Giving each creature a backstory or a purpose can add depth and intrigue to the portfolio. This can be achieved through the use of symbolism, symbolism, or incorporating elements from different cultures or time periods.

As the portfolio progresses, it is important to maintain a cohesive theme or style throughout the collection. This can be achieved by using consistent color palettes, artistic techniques, or visual motifs. A well-curated portfolio that showcases a consistent artistic vision can leave a lasting impression on viewers and potential clients.

Building a portfolio of monster drawings is not just about creating visually striking artwork, but also about showcasing one's creativity, imagination, and technical skills. It is a process that requires dedication, practice, and a willingness to push artistic boundaries. By carefully planning and executing each drawing, an artist can create a portfolio that not only demonstrates their talent but also tells a captivating story through the world of monsters.

Introduction

Kids have this intense desire to express themselves the ways they know how to. During their formative years, drawing all sorts is on top of their favorite things to do. You ought to encourage as it boosts their creativity and generally advances their cognitive development.

This book is written to give you and your kids the smoothest drawing experience with the different guides and instructions on how to draw different kinds of objects and animals. However, you should note that drawing, like everything worthwhile, requires a great deal of patience and consistency. Be patient with your kids as they wade through the tips and techniques in this book and put them into practice. Now, they will not get everything on the first try, but do not let this deter them. Be by their side at every step of the way and gently encourage them. In no time, they will be perfect little creators, and you, their trainer.

Besides, this is a rewarding activity to do as it presents you the opportunity of hanging out with your kids and connecting with them in ways you never knew was possible. The book contains all the help you need, now sit down with them and help them do this.

That is pretty much all about it - we should start this exciting journey now, shouldn't we?

How to Draw a Goblin

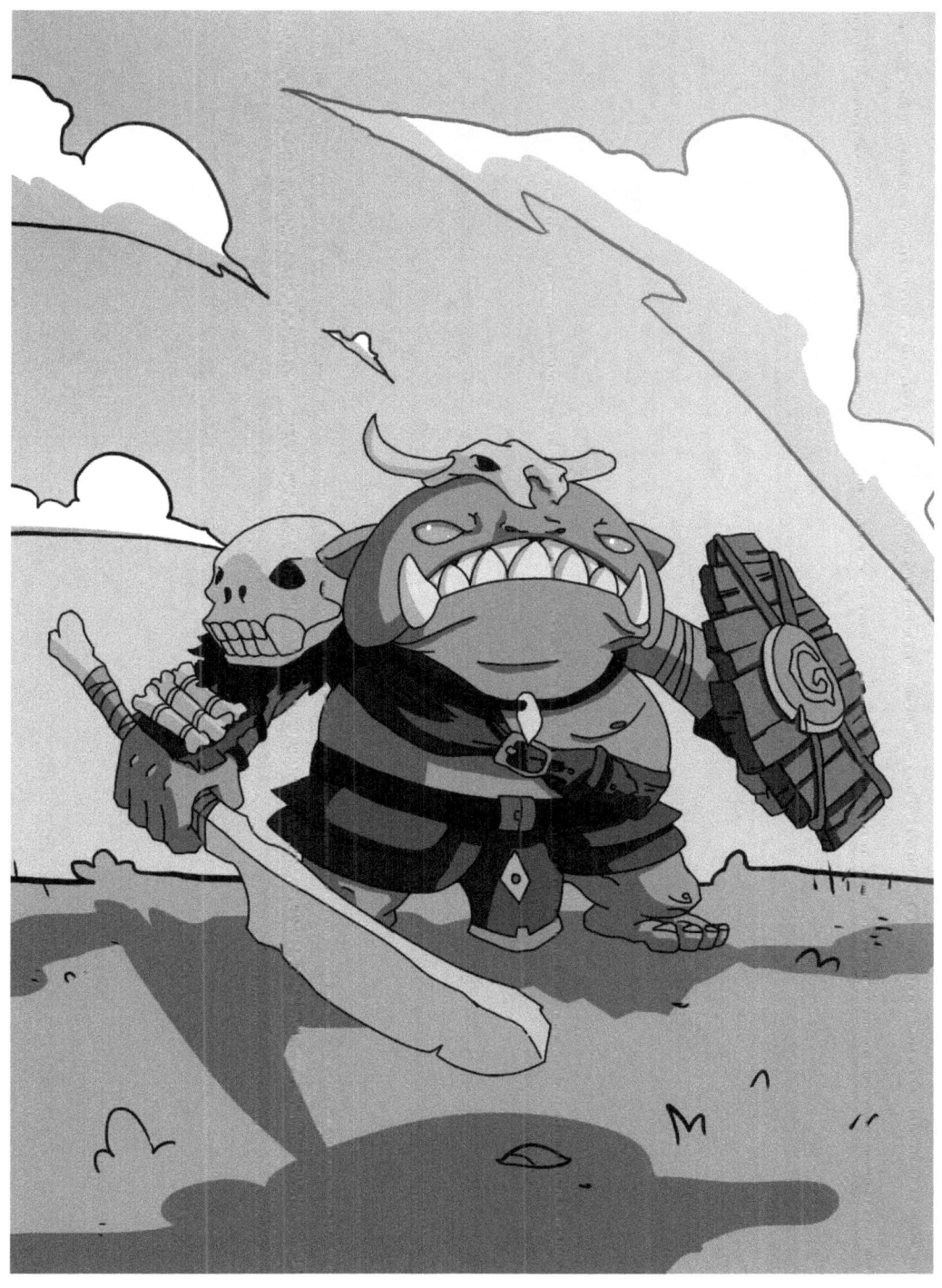

Step 1.

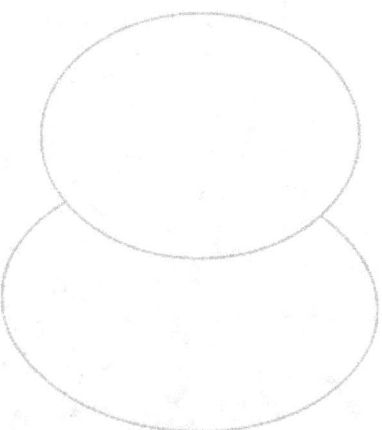

Draw two circles laying on top of each other.

Step 2.

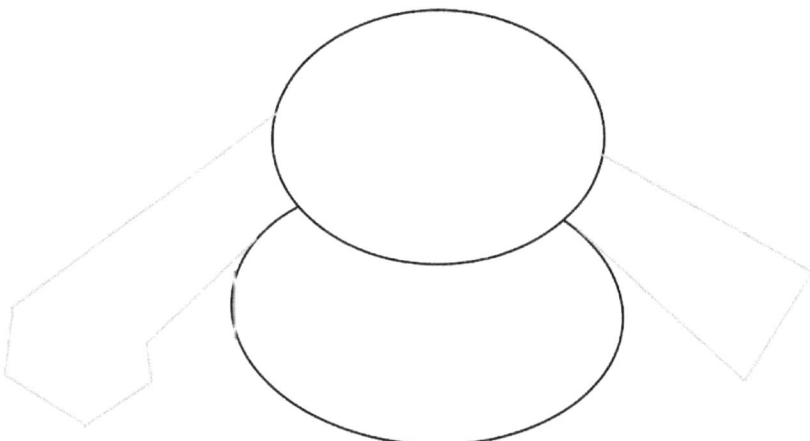

Add two rectangular shapes on each side for the arms.

Step 3.

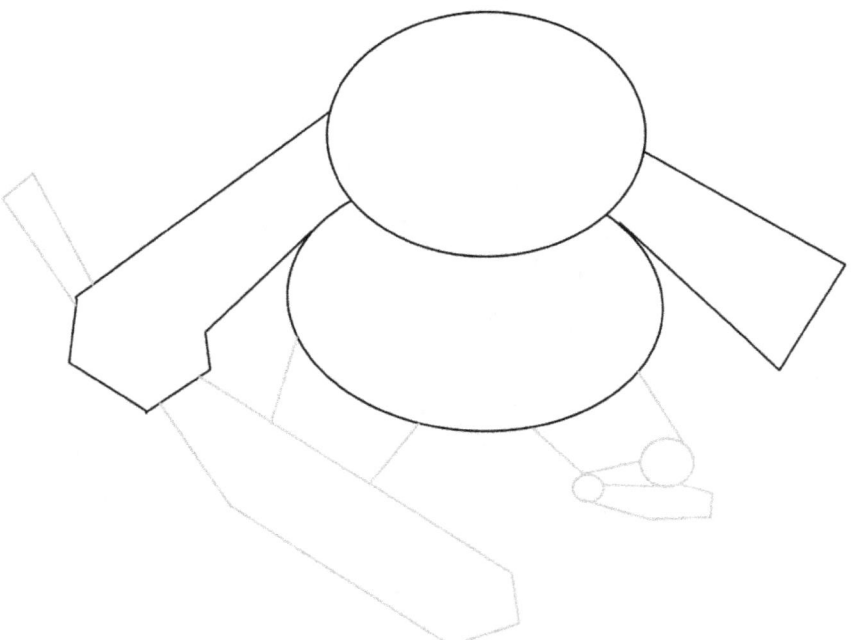

Add the outline of the sword to his right hand.
Then add the outline of the legs.
Notice that his right leg is hidden behind the sword.
His left legs has two circles for the joints. Don't forget the outline of his foot.

Step 4.

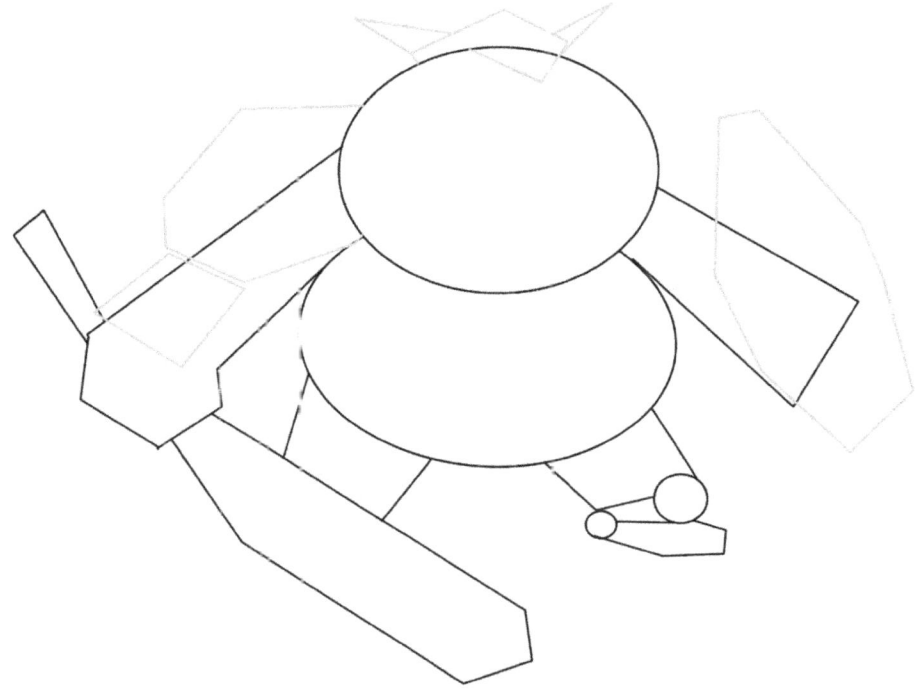

Add the outline of the shield to the left hand.
Add the skeleton helmet.
Then add the shoulder pad and the lower arm pad to the right arm.

Step 5.

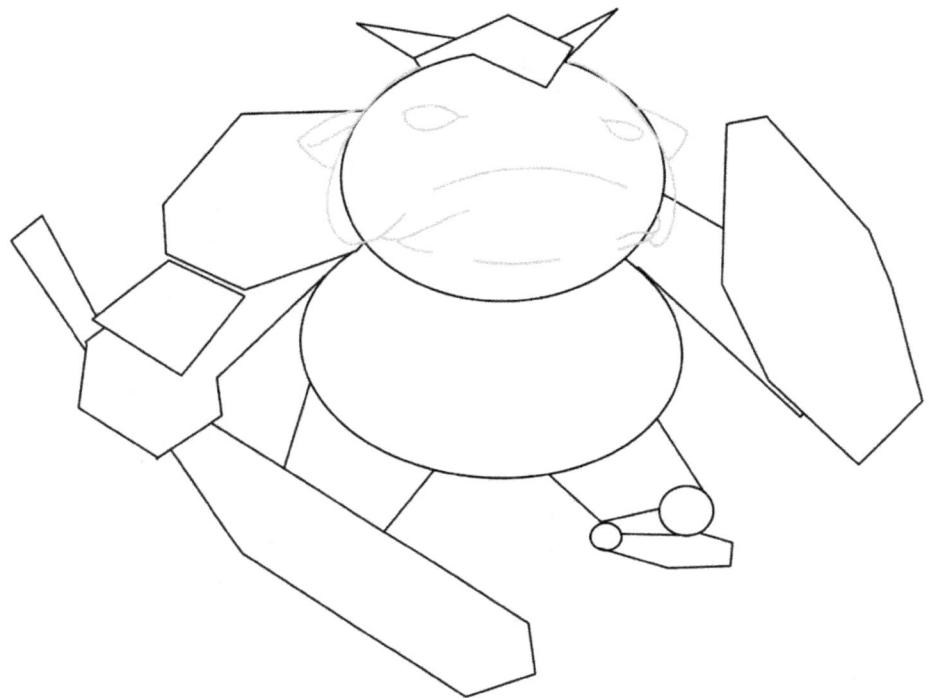

Redraw the face to give it the cheeks of a bulldog.
Add the outline of the chin and add his ears to the side of the head.
Then add a mean look line for the lips and add the eyes.

Step 6.

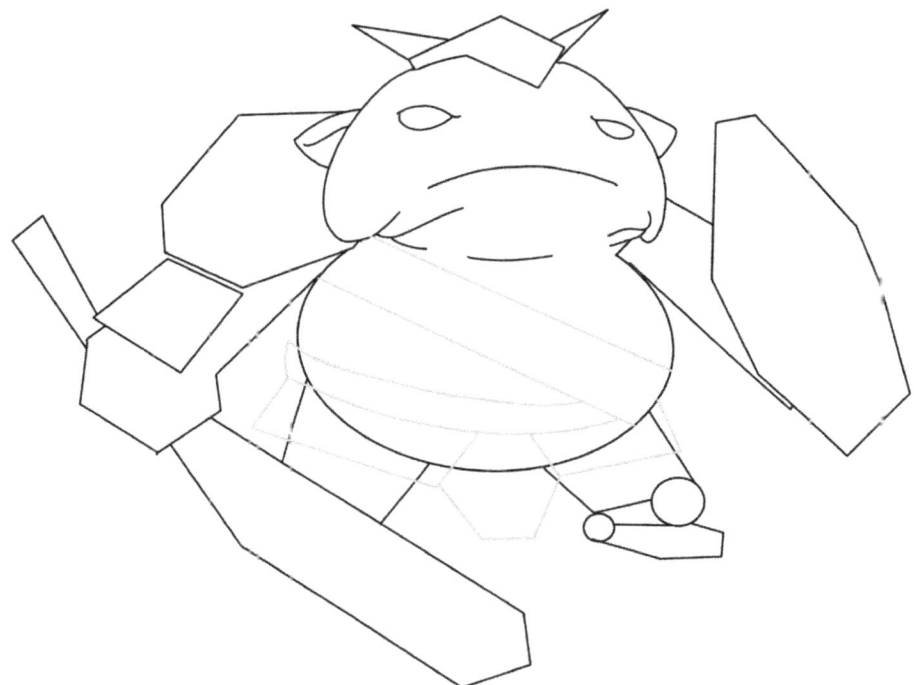

Add two lines across the chest for the chest band.
Add a belt and the armor to protect the upper legs and groin.

Step 7.

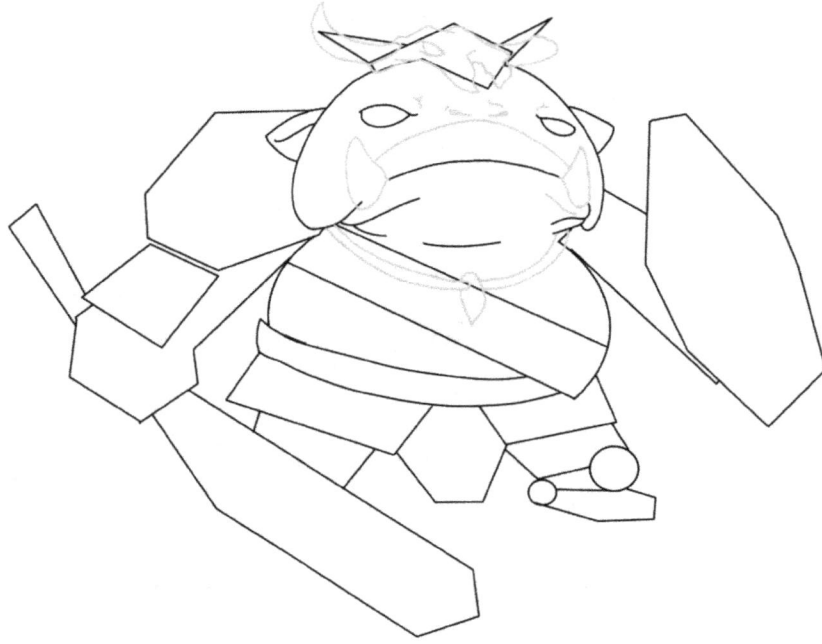

Redraw the skeleton helmet to make the horns and the skull. Make one of the horns broken.
Use the example to help you along.
Add a flat nose in between the eyes and some lines for the eyebrows.
Add two large fangs to each side of the mouth.
Then add another line to show an open mouth.
Now go down to his neck to draw the necklace with the tooth in the center of it.

Step 8.

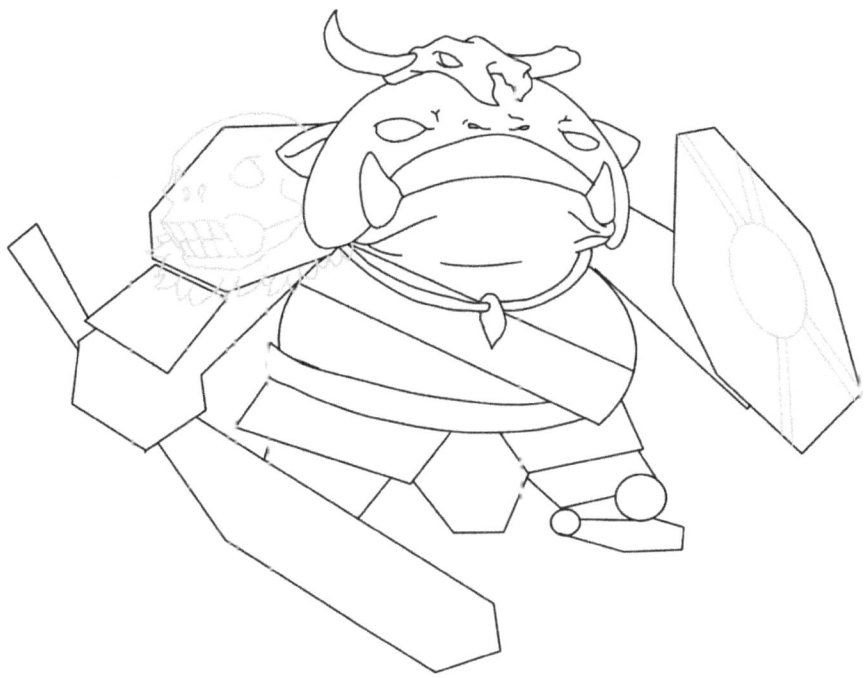

Add a circle to the center of the shield.
Then add four strands pointing to each corner of the shield.
The shoulder pad is up next.
Draw a skull in its place. Make sure to give it a nice fur bed so it doesn't hurt the shoulder.

Step 9.

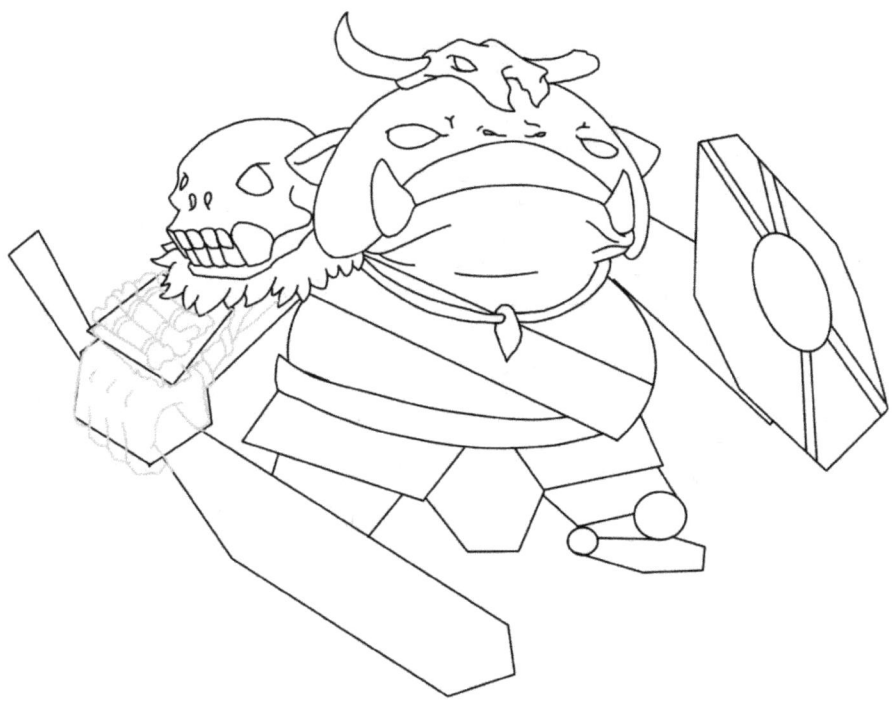

Now for his right arm.
Redraw it to give it more volume.
Then add a fur bed to his arm and draw three bones on top of it.
Connect it to the arm by drawing two strands on the inside.
Then redraw the hand and make the fingers bend around the sword.

Step 10.

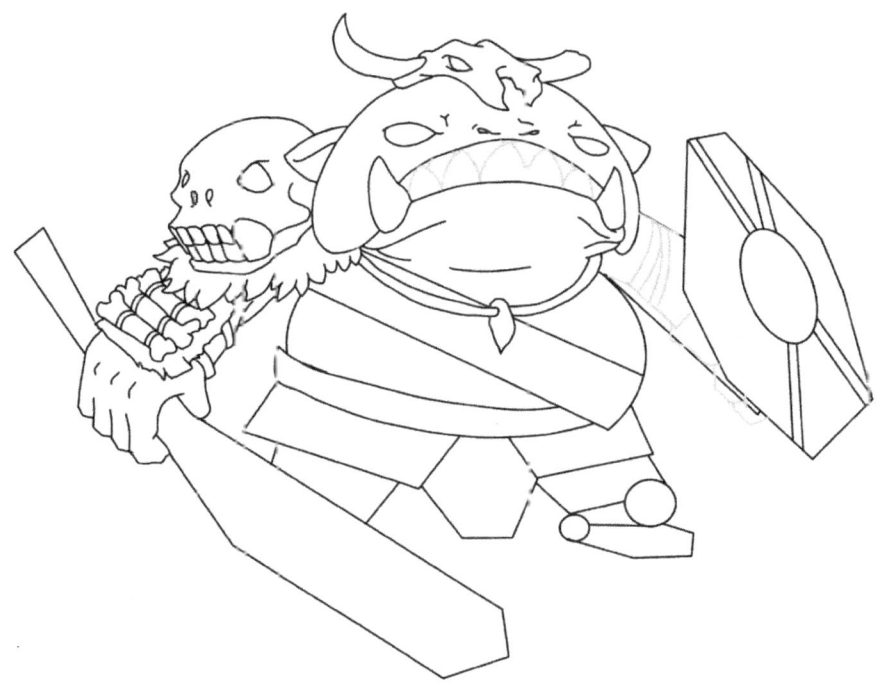

Add a row of sharp teeth to his mouth.
Then redraw the visible part of the left arm.
Add cloth to the arm to show where he had a wound.
Add a wrist band and draw the thumb and finger.

Step 11.

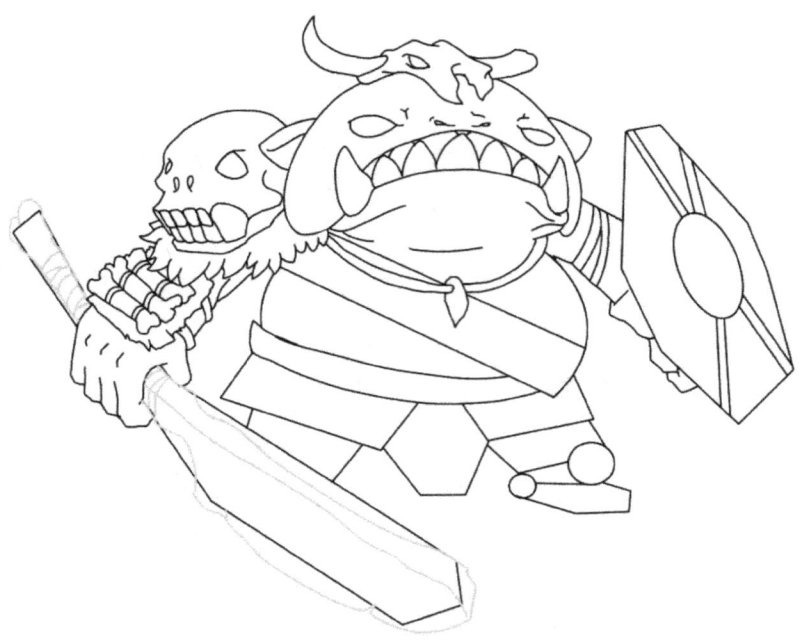

Let's redraw his bone sword.
The back of the sword has a normal bone sticking out.
The front is shaped in the form of a blunt blade.
Make yours however creative you want it to be. I kept it simple so show that he isn't the smartest Goblin. If it works, it's not stupid!
Add some lines of cloth along the handle so that he doesn't hurt himself when grabbing it.

Step 12.

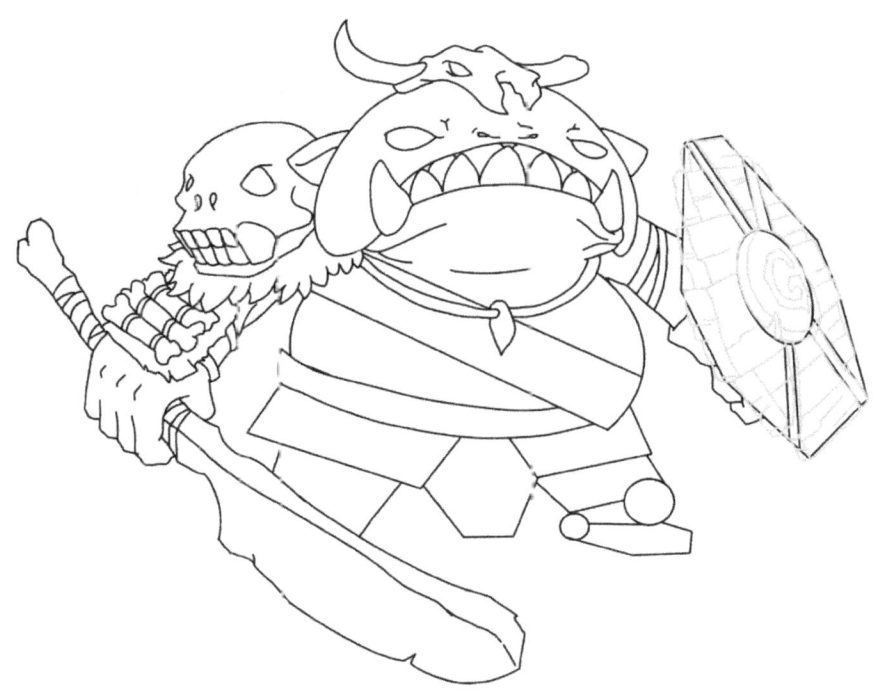

Now for the shield.
Add horizontally placed wooden planks along the width of the shield.
Make them go from short to long, to short.
Redraw the strands to bend them around the rope.
Then redraw the circle and give it a cool symbol in the middle.

Step 13.

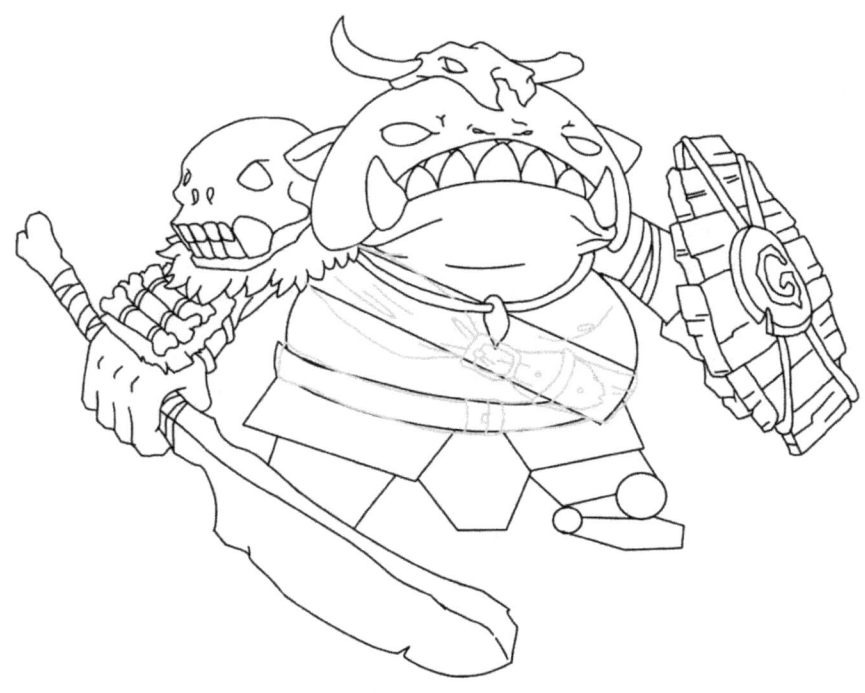

Let's redraw the strap across his chest.
Add a belt buckle to the middle of the strap.
Then redraw the lines to make it a cloth belt, tightly bound with the belt buckle.
Add the outline of his chest and his nipple.
Then redraw the belt and add a belt buckle to its center.

Step 14.

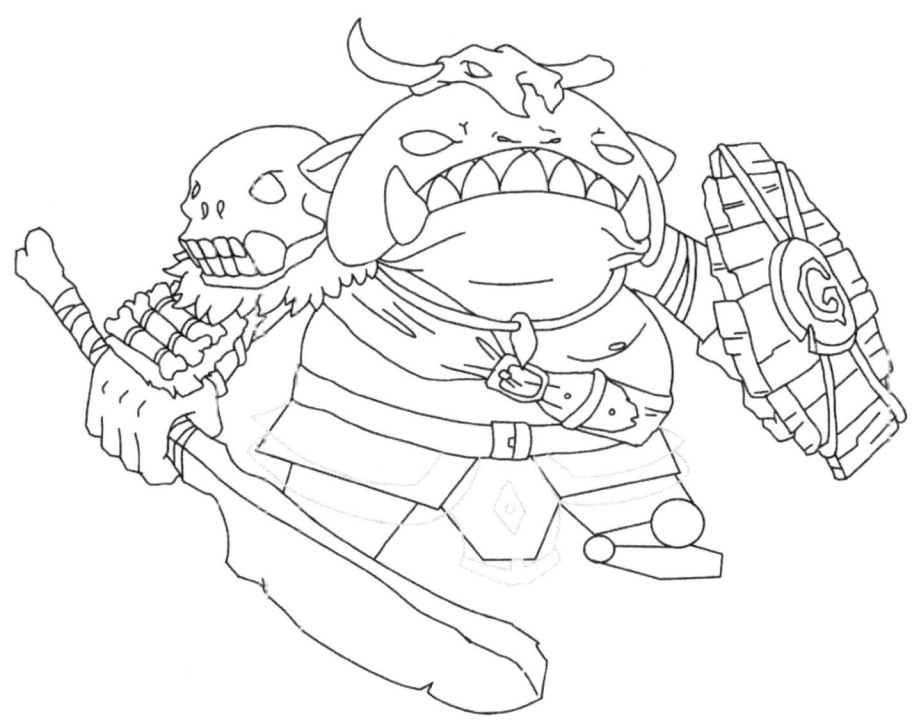

Redraw the leg guards with two plates on each side.
Redraw the groin flap and make it slightly longer than the outline.
Add a cuff to its end and a symbol in the center.

Step 15.

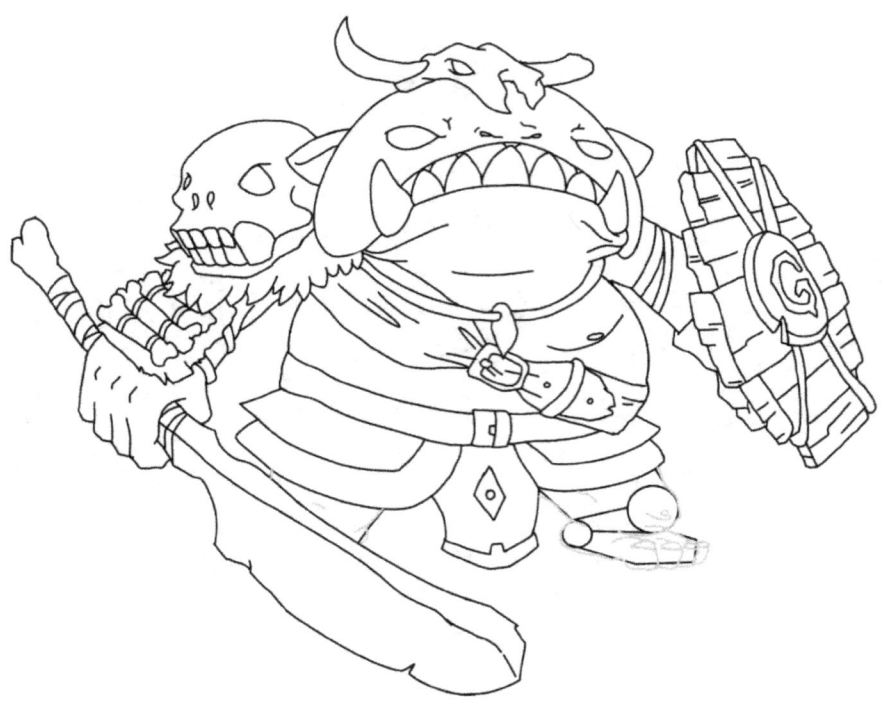

Redraw the legs.
Add some lines to show where the knees are.
Add the toes to the feet.
Notice that from the angle he is standing is, we cannot see the fifth toe.

Step 16.

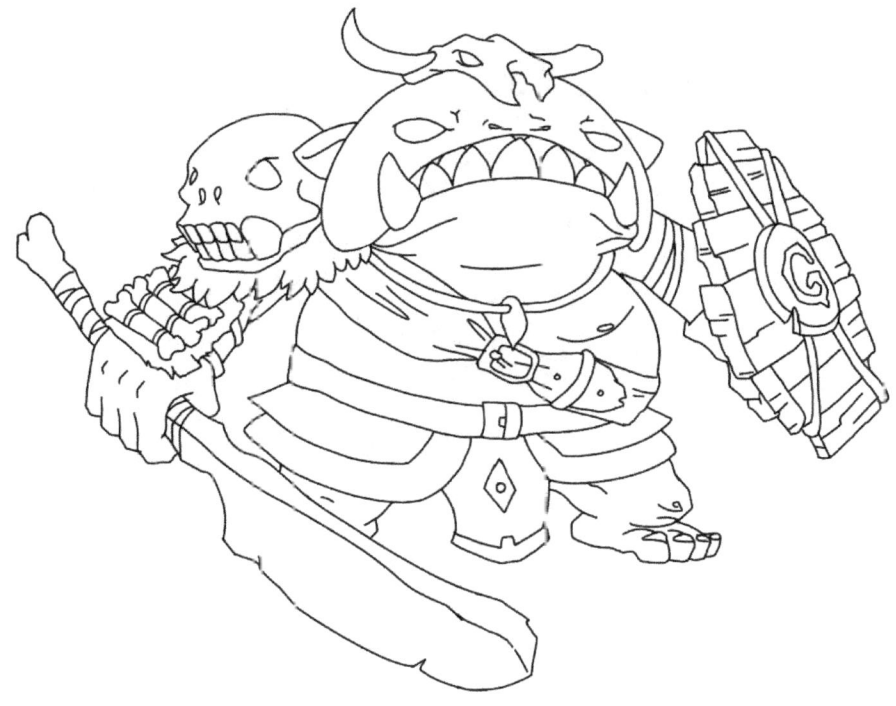

All done! Let's color!

Step 17.

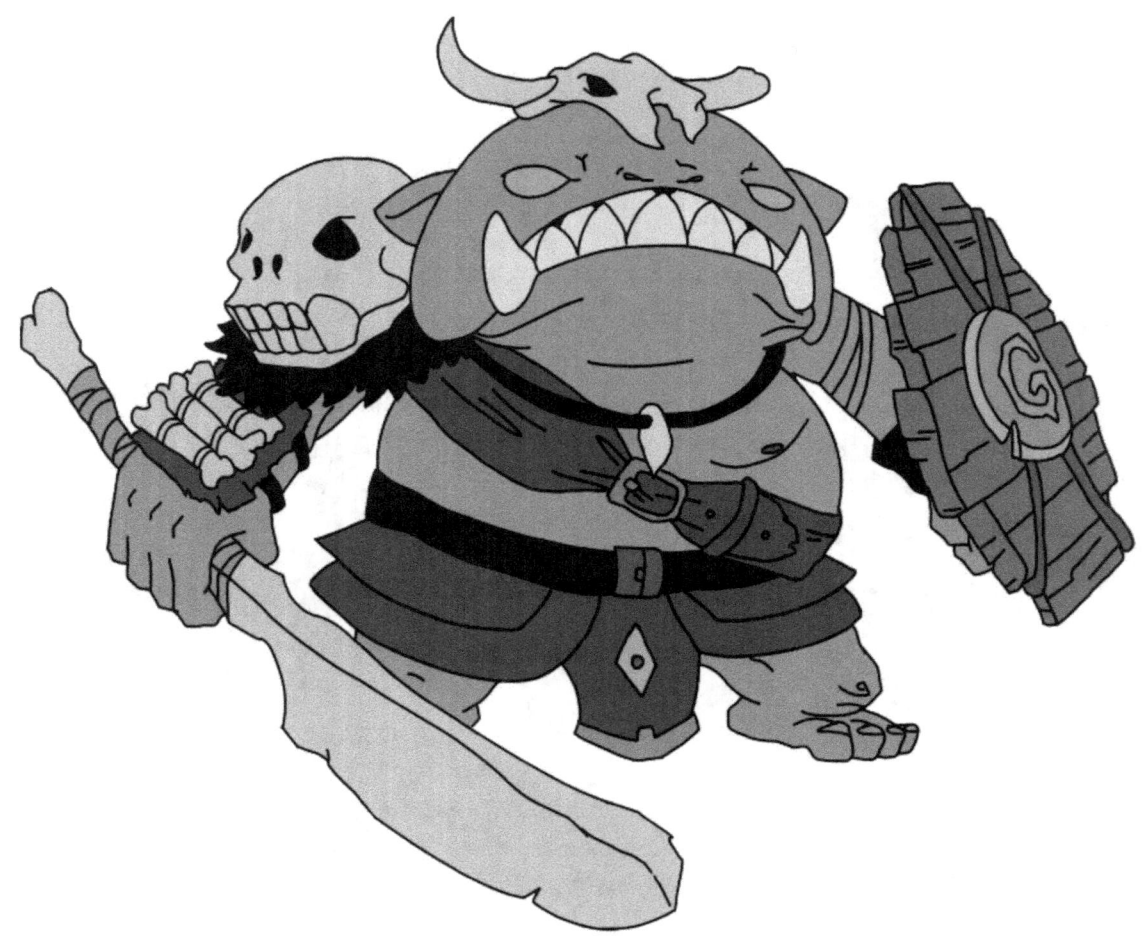

His body is green and his eyes are dark yellow.
The skulls, bones and sword are gray.
Then bandages on the sword and his arm are blue.
The shield is brown, with dark colored straps and a lighter colored center.
The wrist band and the bed on his shoulder are blue.
The bed on his forearm, the belts on his chest and waist, and the groin protection is brown.

The necklace is dark red and the tooth a lighter grey. The teeth are a little yellow.

Step 18.

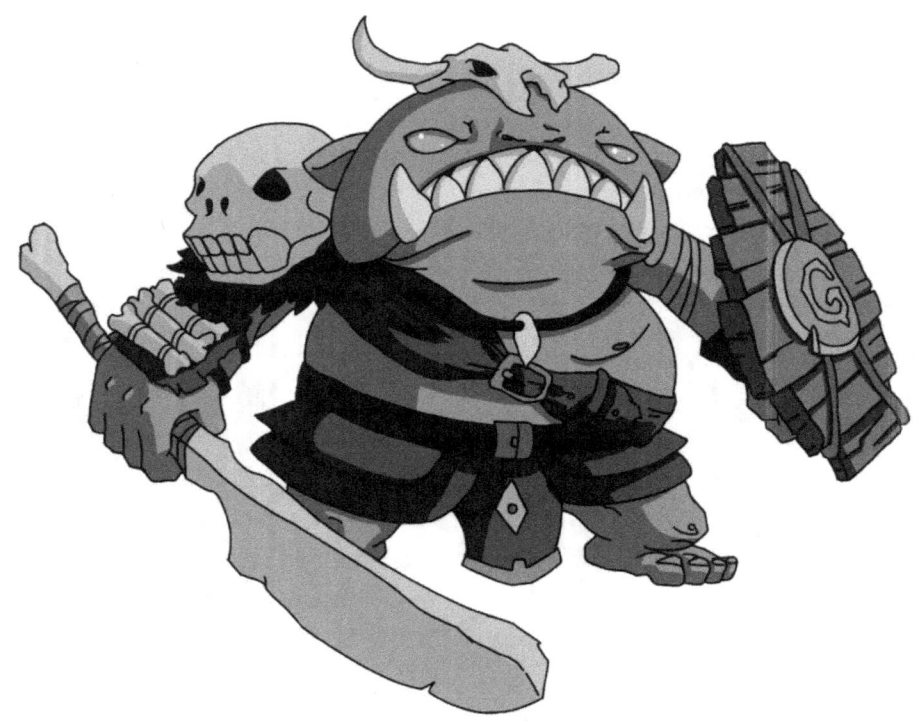

Add some shadow to give him more volume.

Step 19.

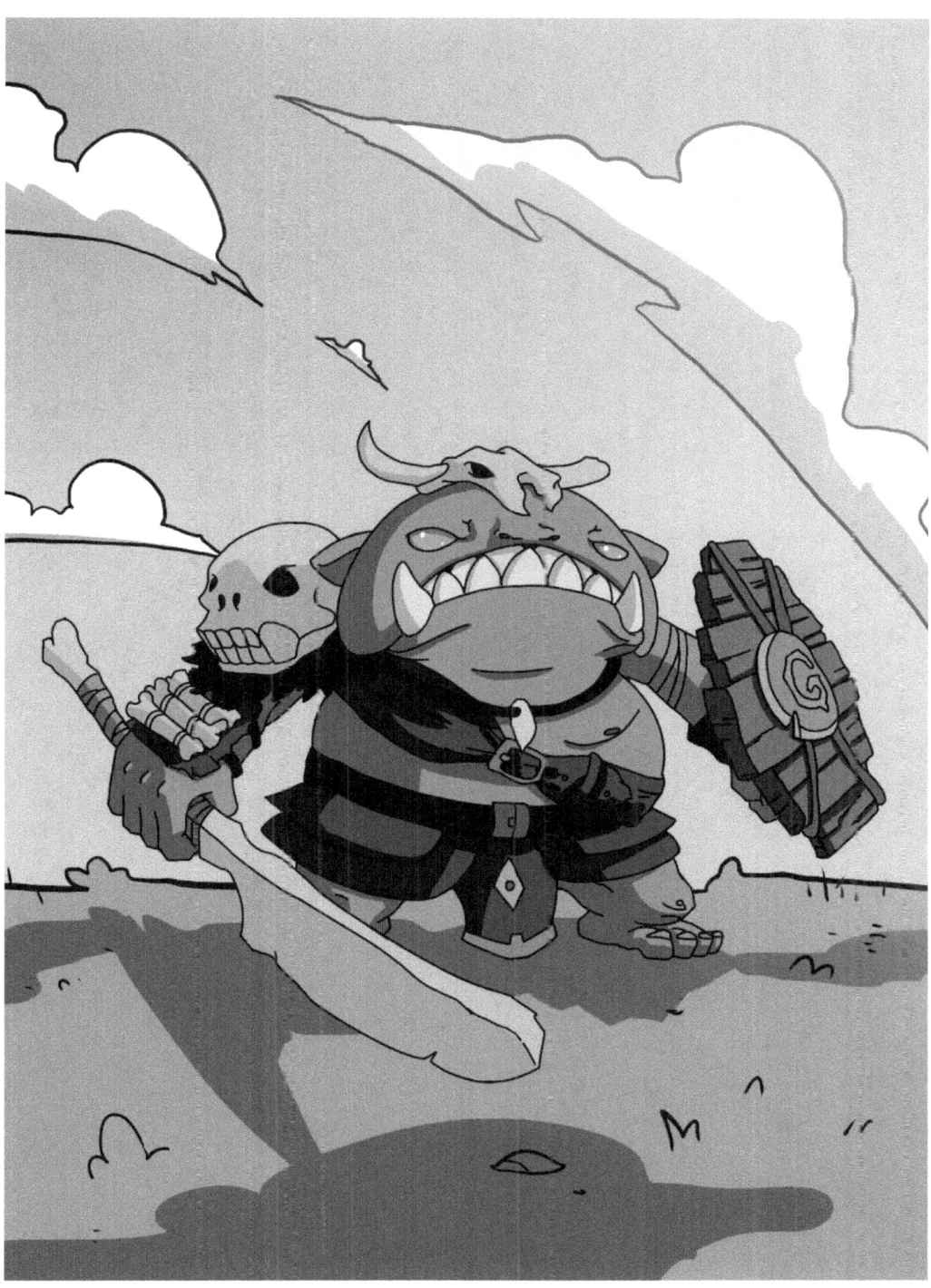

Colored version.

Step 20.

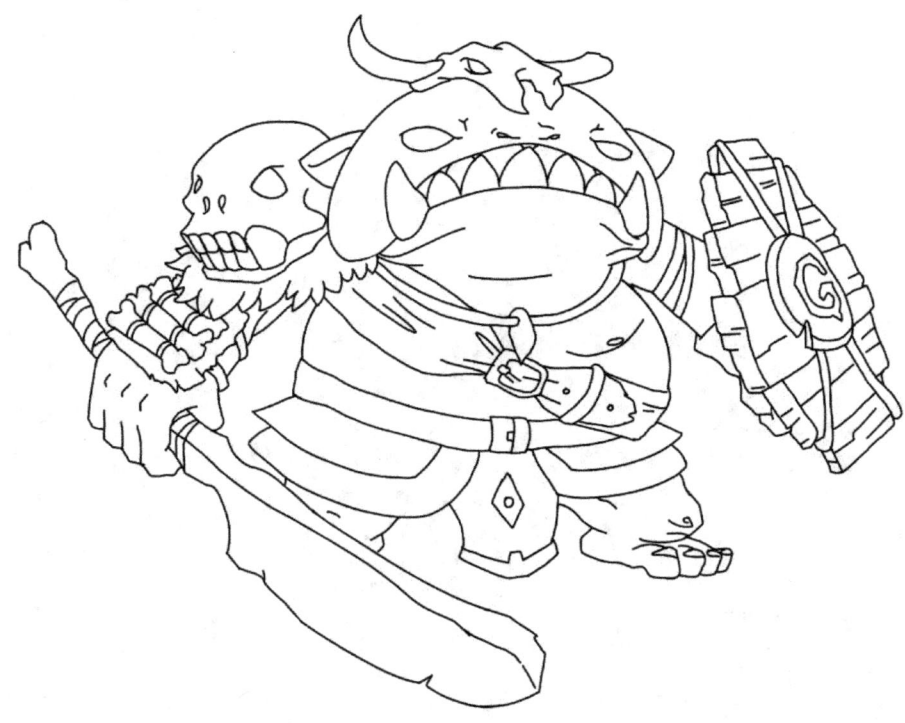

Line art version.

How to Draw a Green Frog

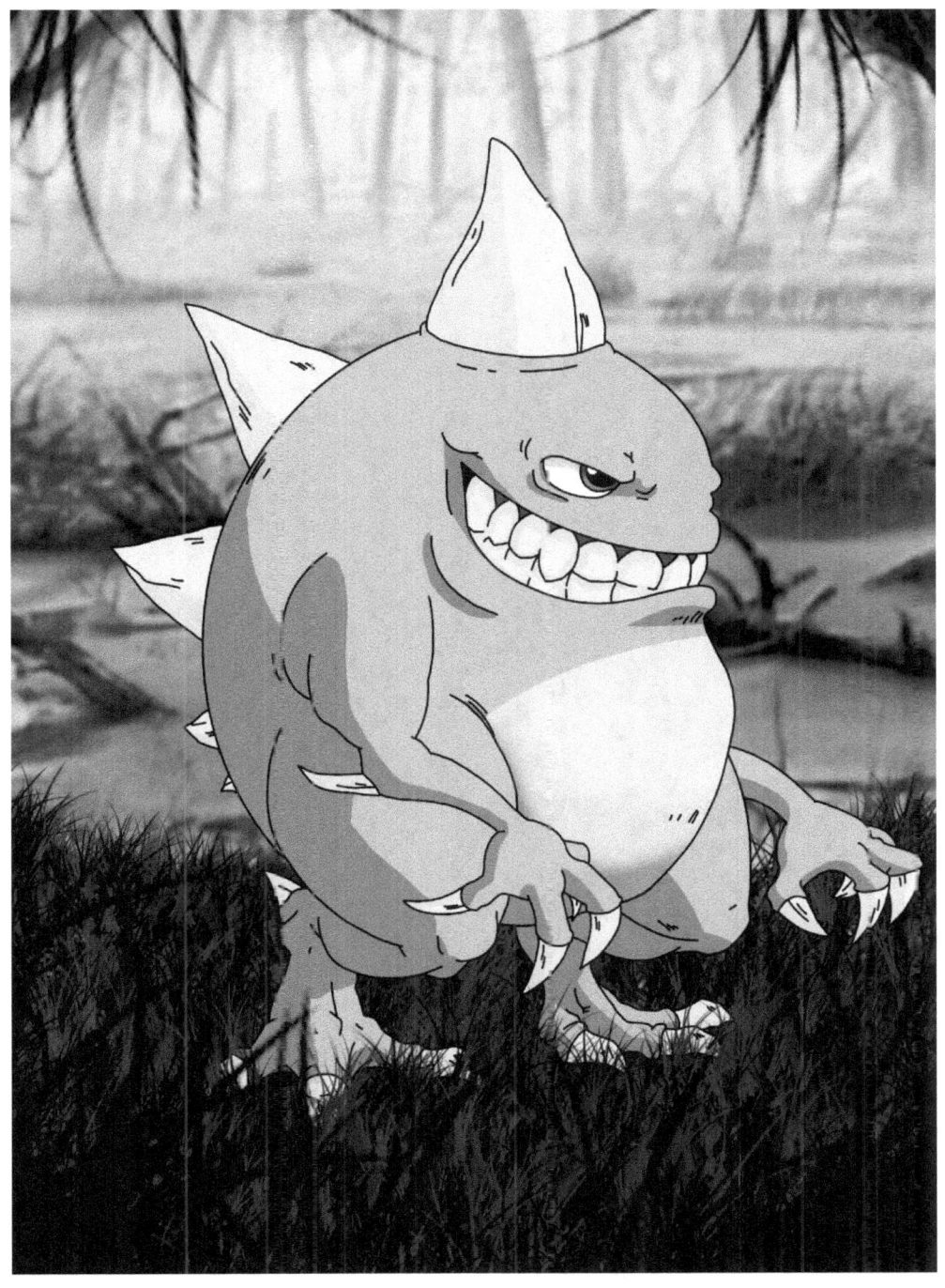

Step 1.

Draw a circle for the body.

Step 2.

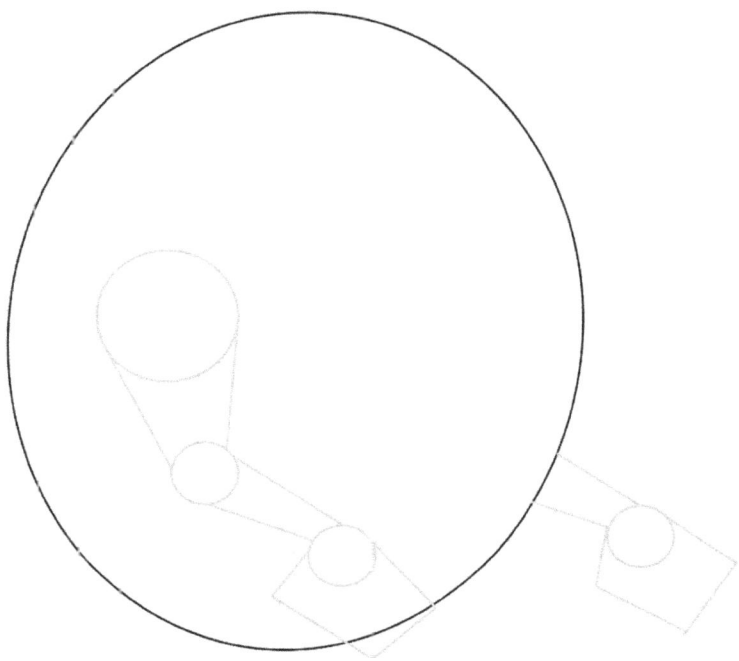

Add circled for the shoulder, elbow and wrists.
Connect them to make the arms and add the outline of the hands.

Step 3.

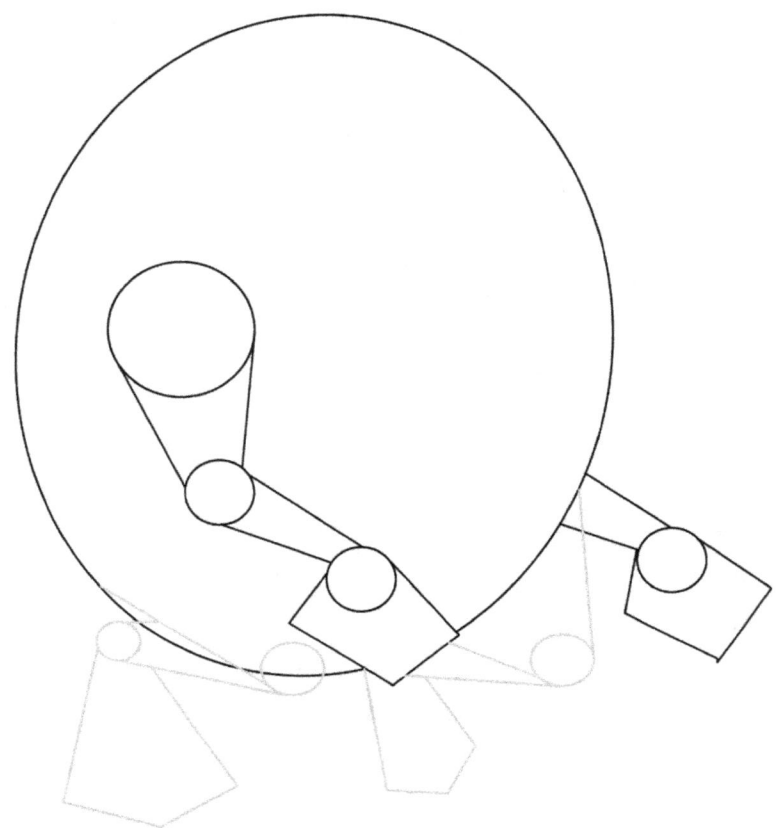

Add circles for the knees and ankles.
Connect them to make the legs and add the outline of the feet.

Step 4.

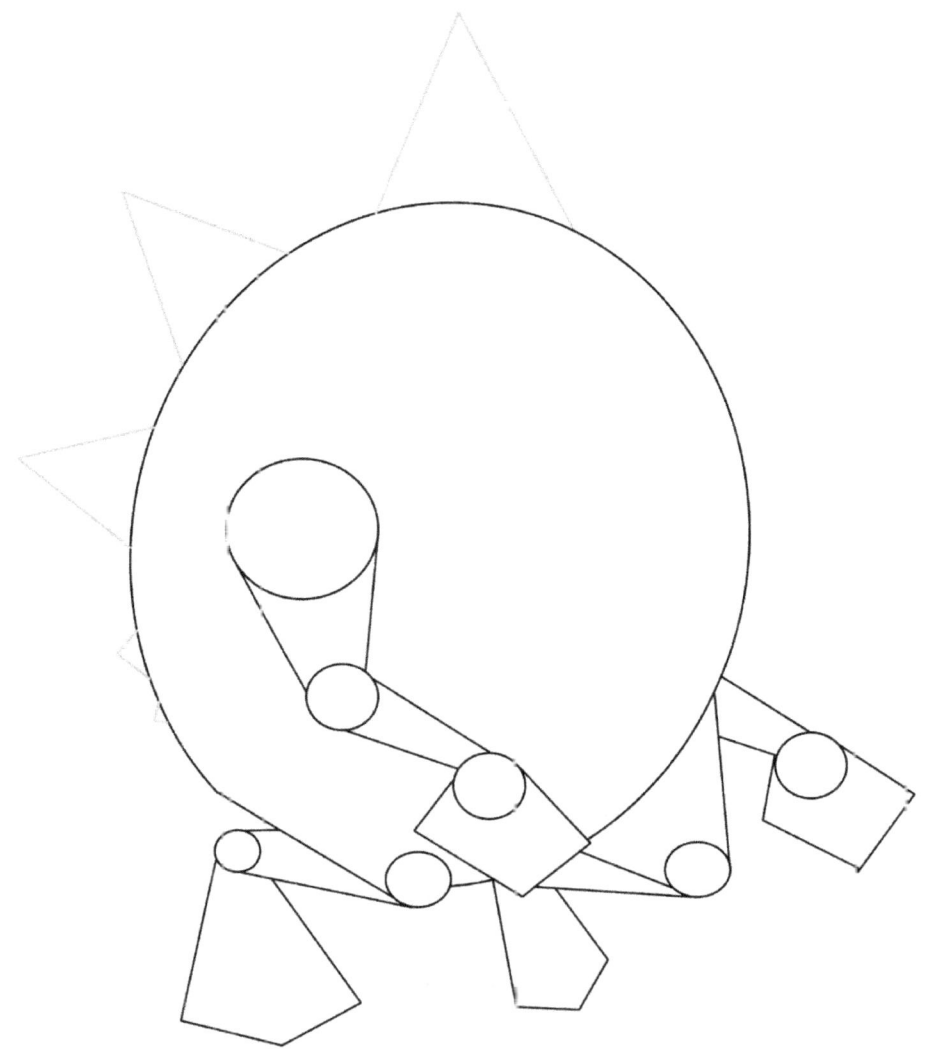

Add 5 spikes on his back, going from large to smaller.

Step 5.

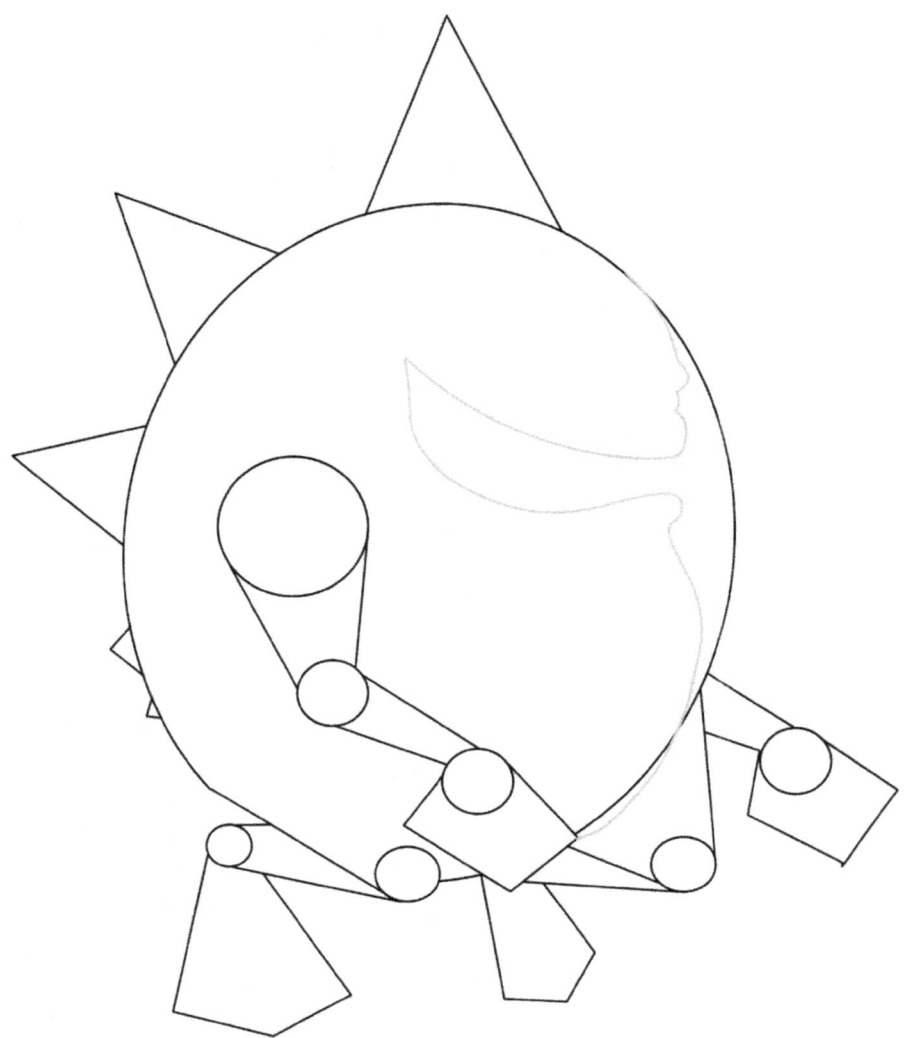

Redraw the face to give it a pointy smile, lips and a curved belly.

Step 6.

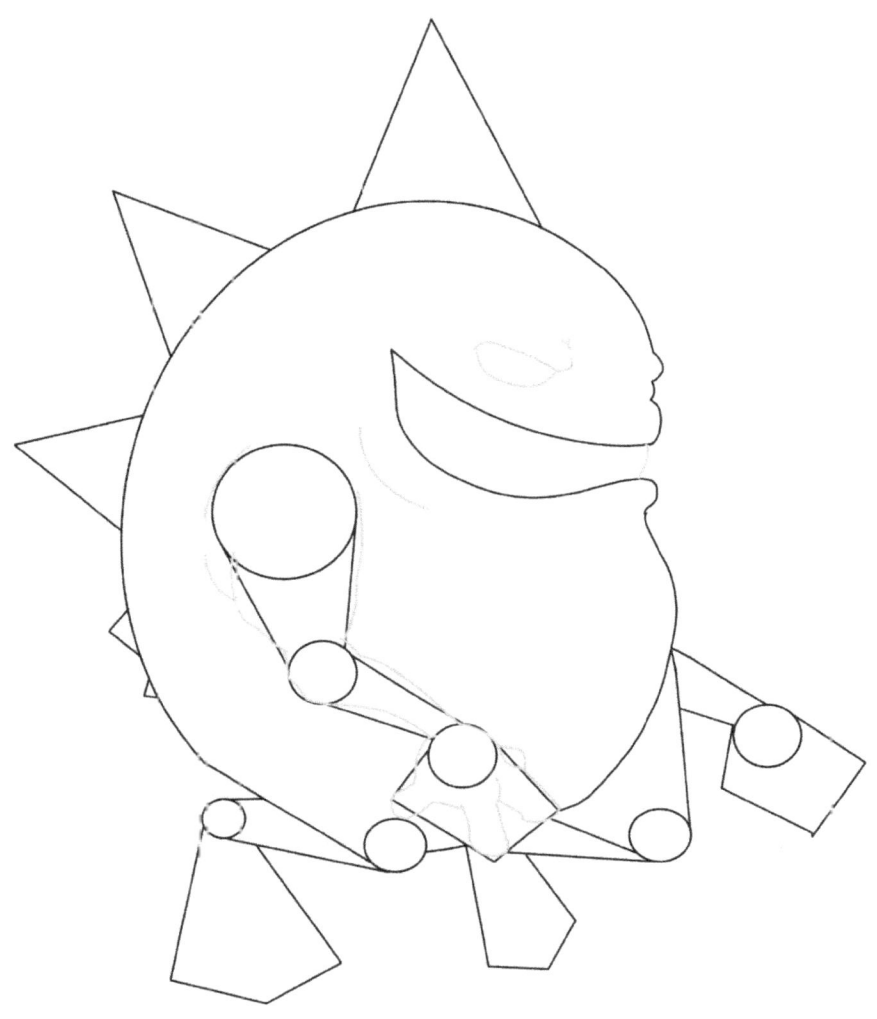

Add and evil looking eye to the head.
Add a line inside the mouth for the end of the teeth, and a line to the side of the mouth to show where the skin folds.
Now redraw his arm. He is a frog so don't worry about making a flabby arm.
Add three fingers to his hand.

Step 7.

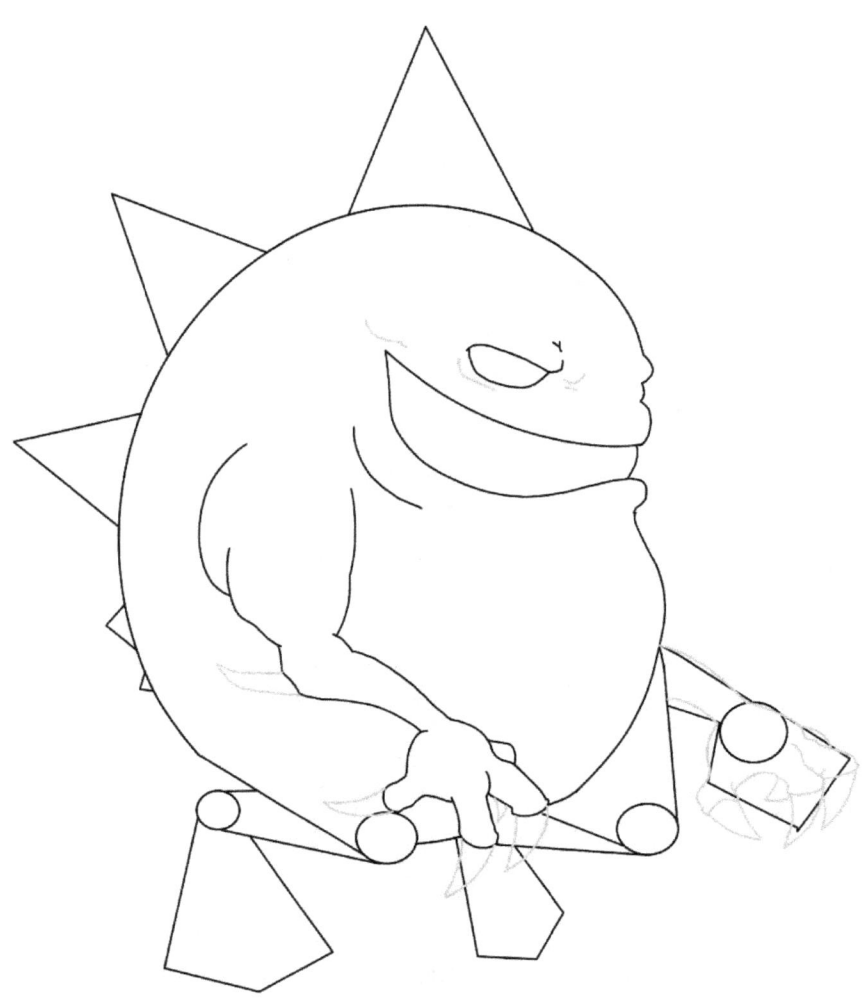

Add sharp nails to the hand and a sharp spike to the elbow.
Now redraw his left hand and make the sharp finger nails.

Step 8.

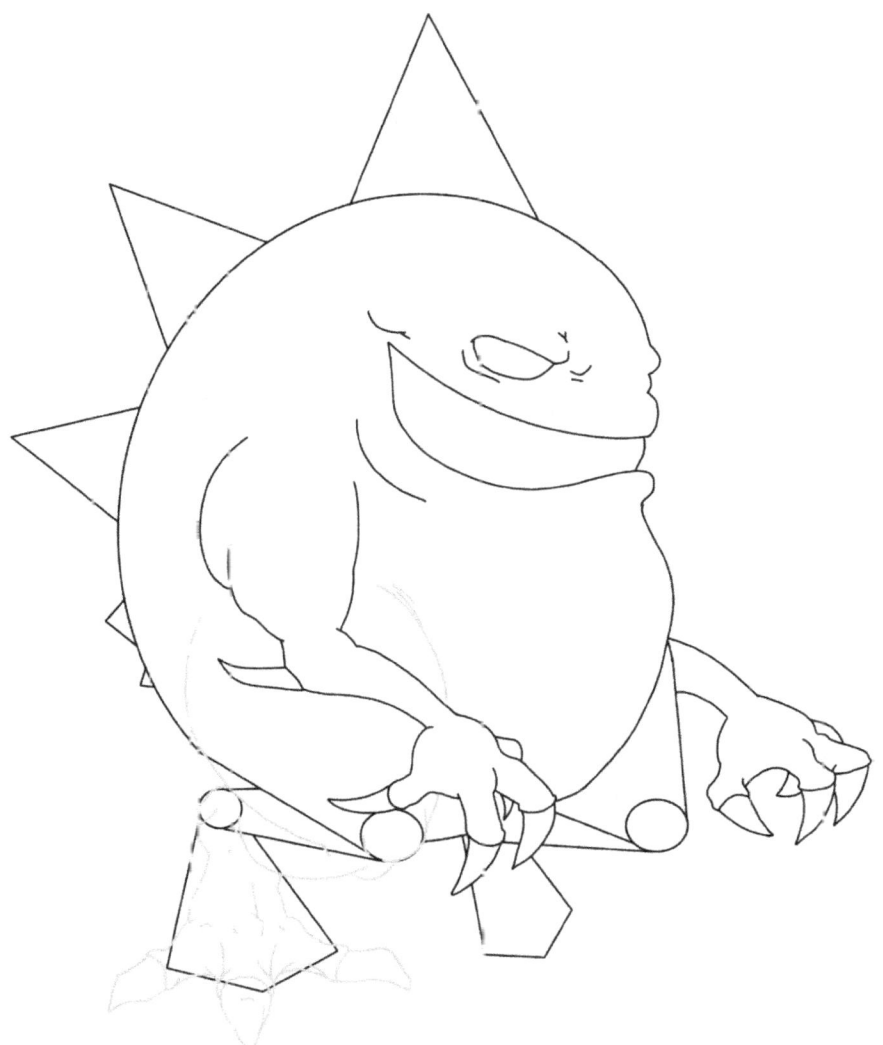

Continue with his right leg.
His leg begins higher up on his body as in the example.
Don't worry about making the leg a little fat.
Bend it back words and add the three toes to his foot.
Then add some sharp nails to the toes.

Step 9.

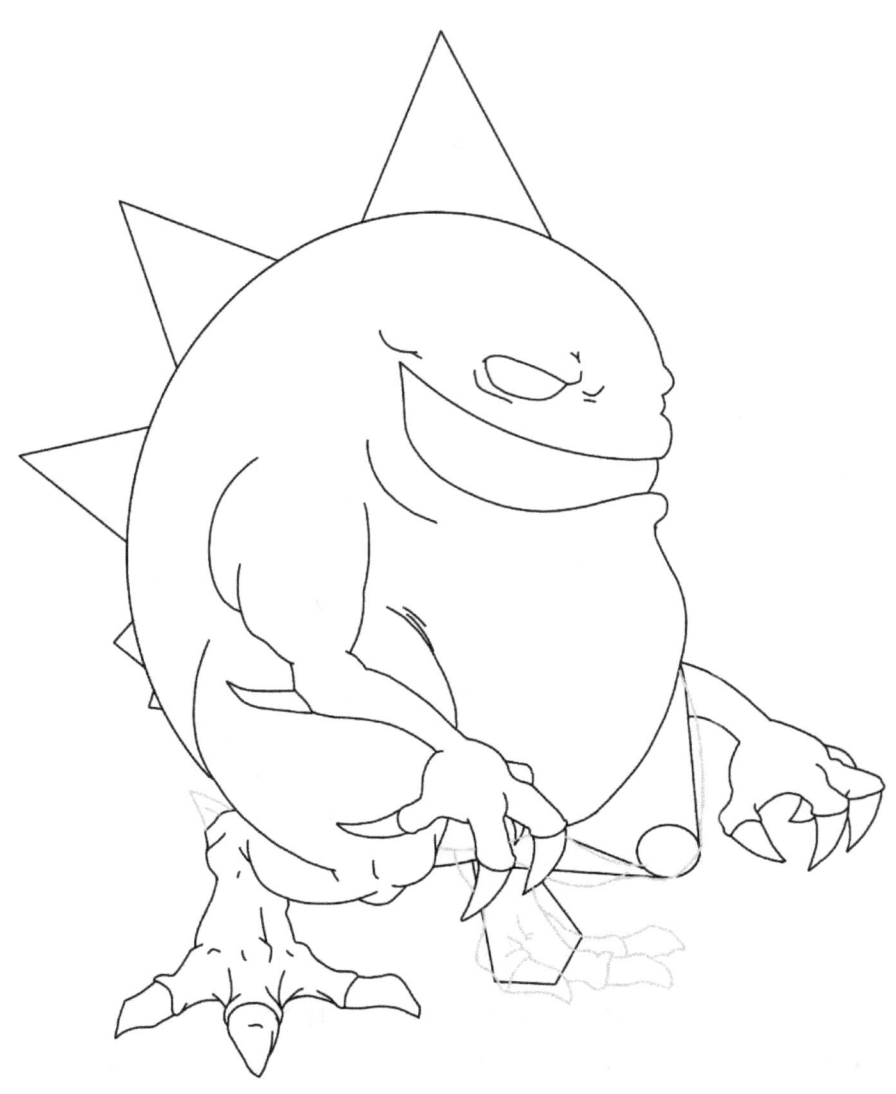

Do the same for the left leg.
Make sure to use the example to help you make the legs.

Step 10.

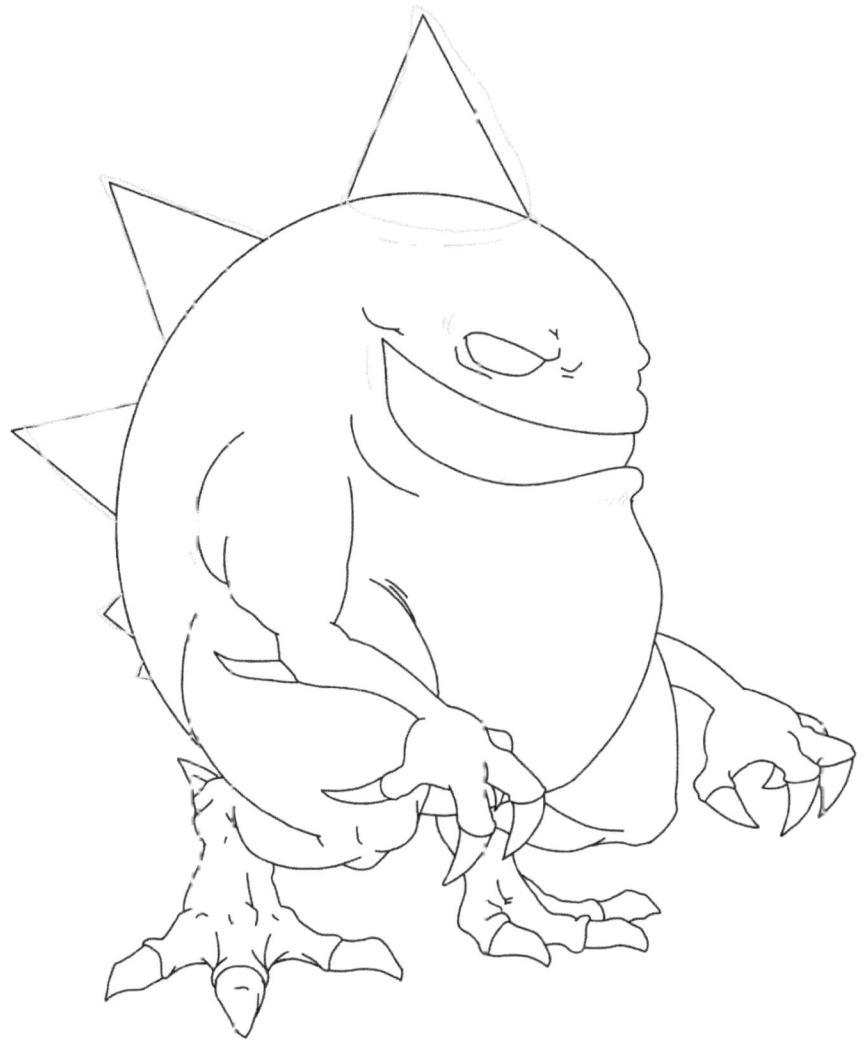

Redraw the spikes on his back and give them some rough edges.
Make sure you use the example to see how to add the big spike to his scalp.
Add some extra lines to the face for details.

Step 11.

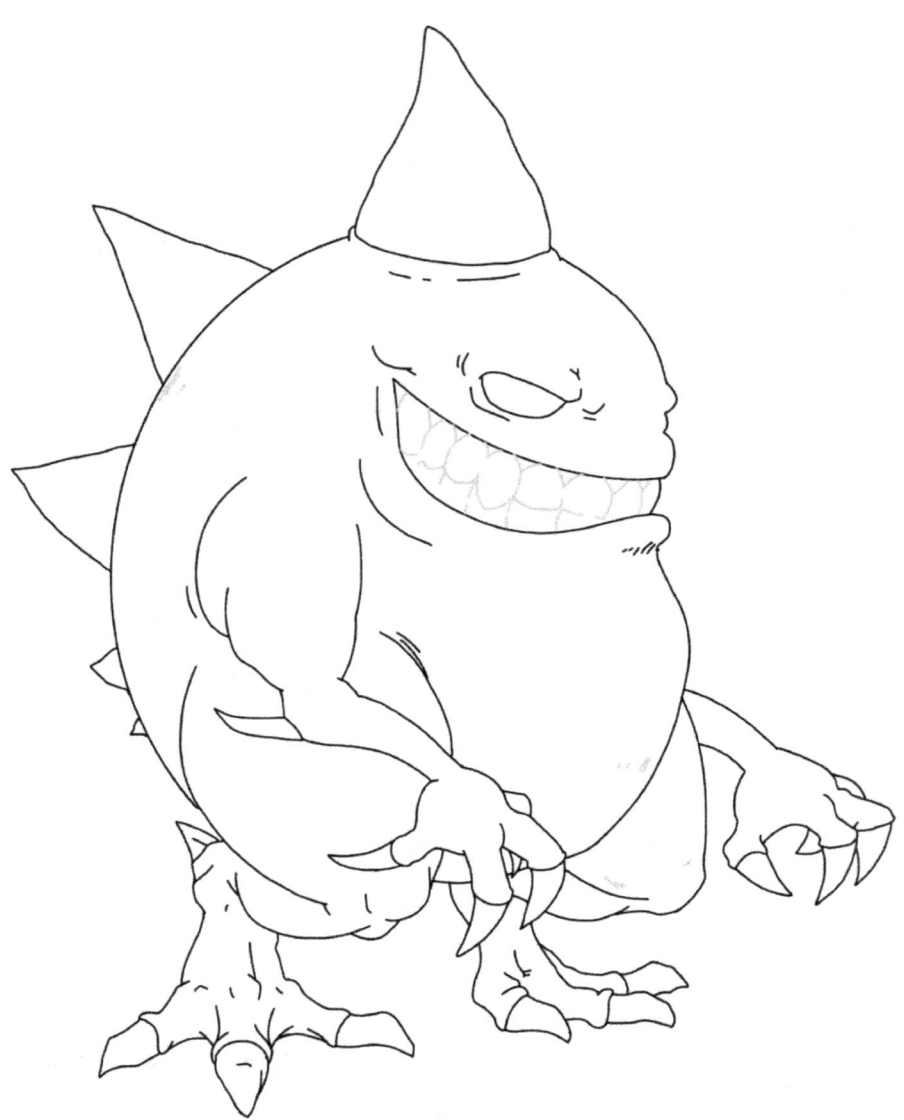

Add some mean looking but big teeth to his mouth. Make sure you show some gum.
Then add some lines across the body for extra detail.

Step 12.

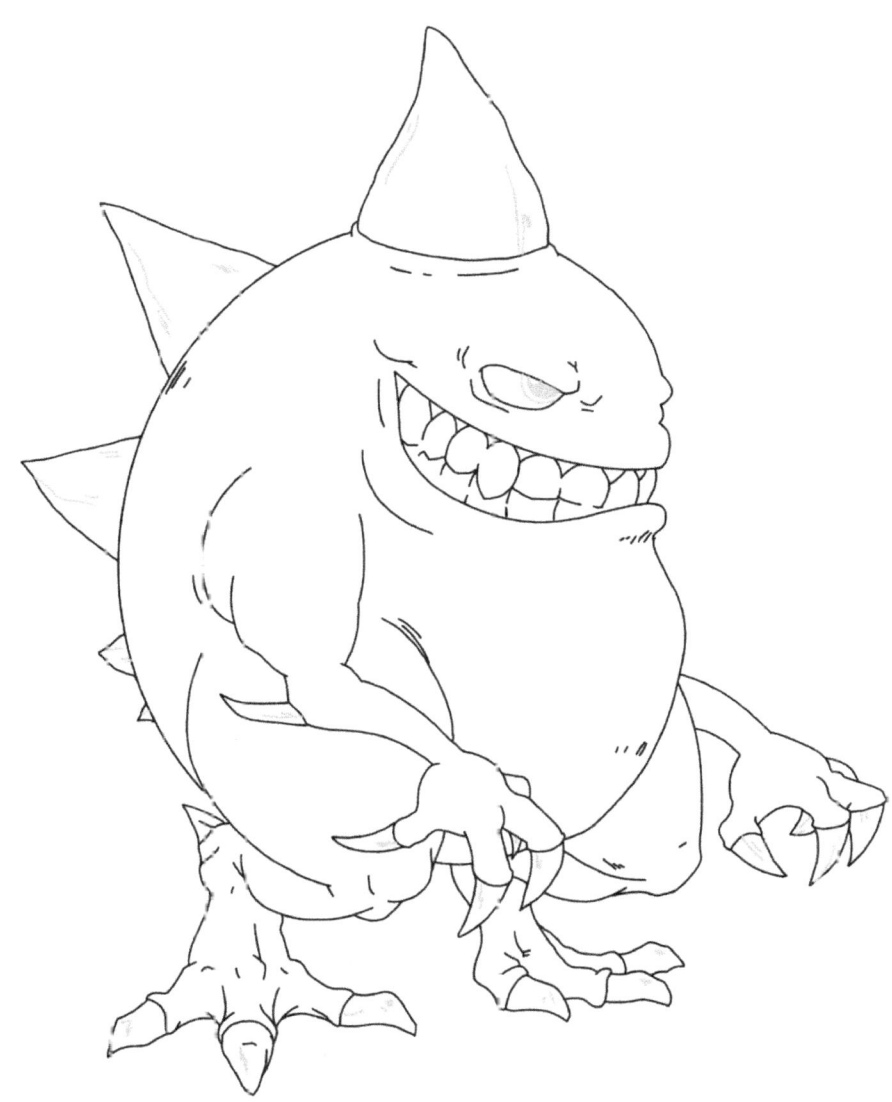

Continue with adding lines to the bigger shapes of the body, such as the spikes and the nails.
Then add a pupil with a large iris to the eyeball.

Step 13.

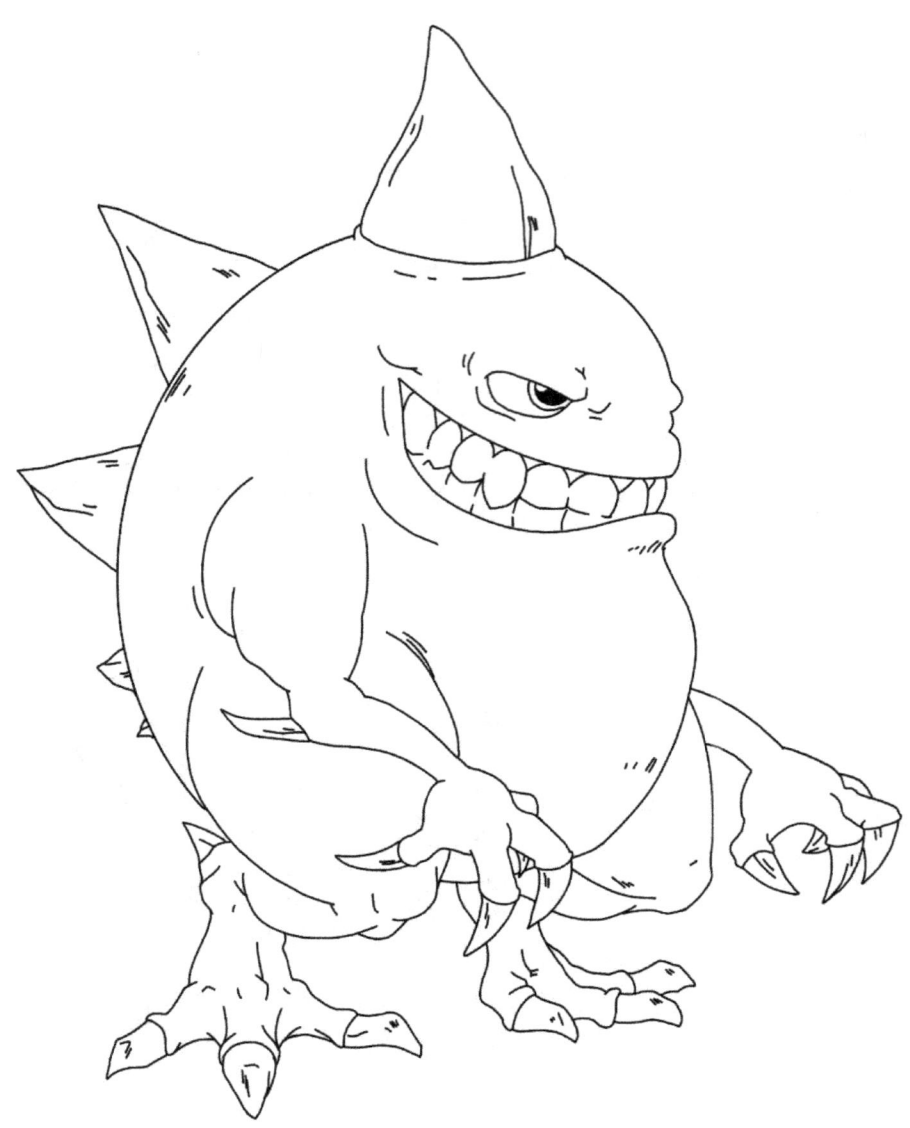

All done! Let's color!

Step 14.

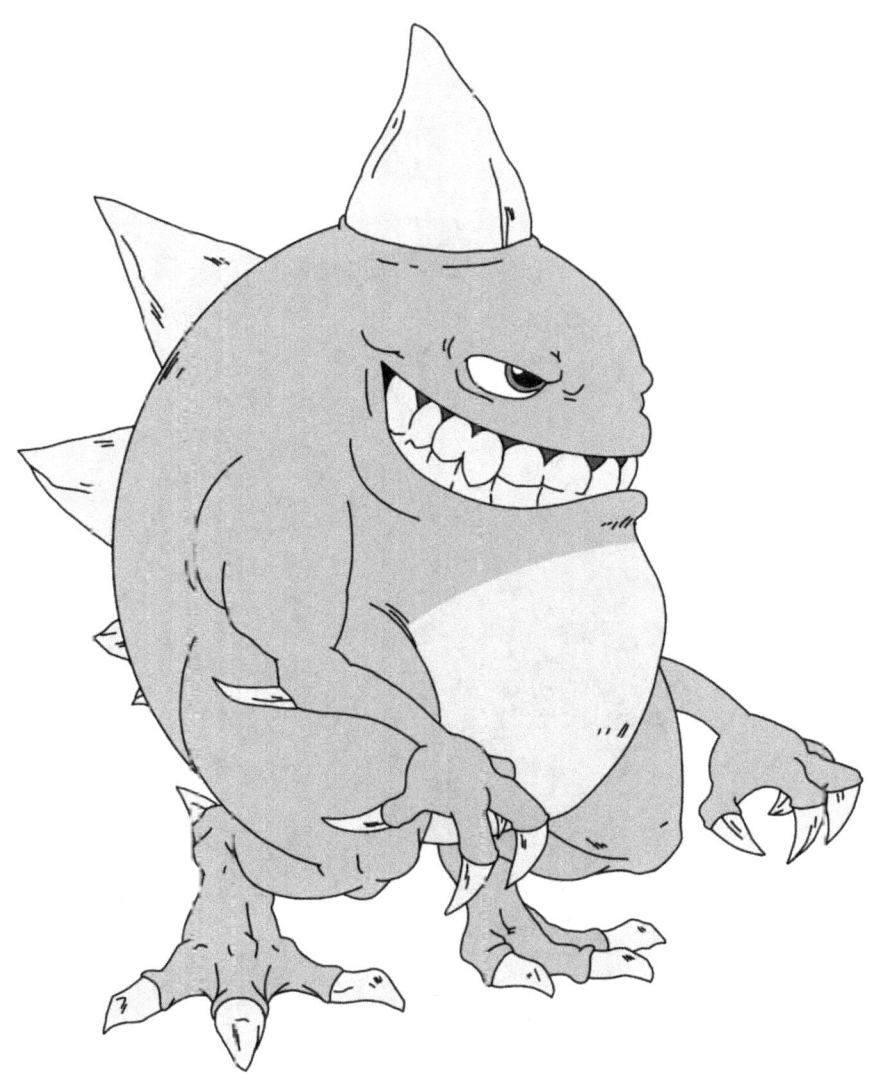

His body is green and his eyes are dark red.
The spikes and the nails are a very light orange.
The belly has a lighter green area.

Step 15.

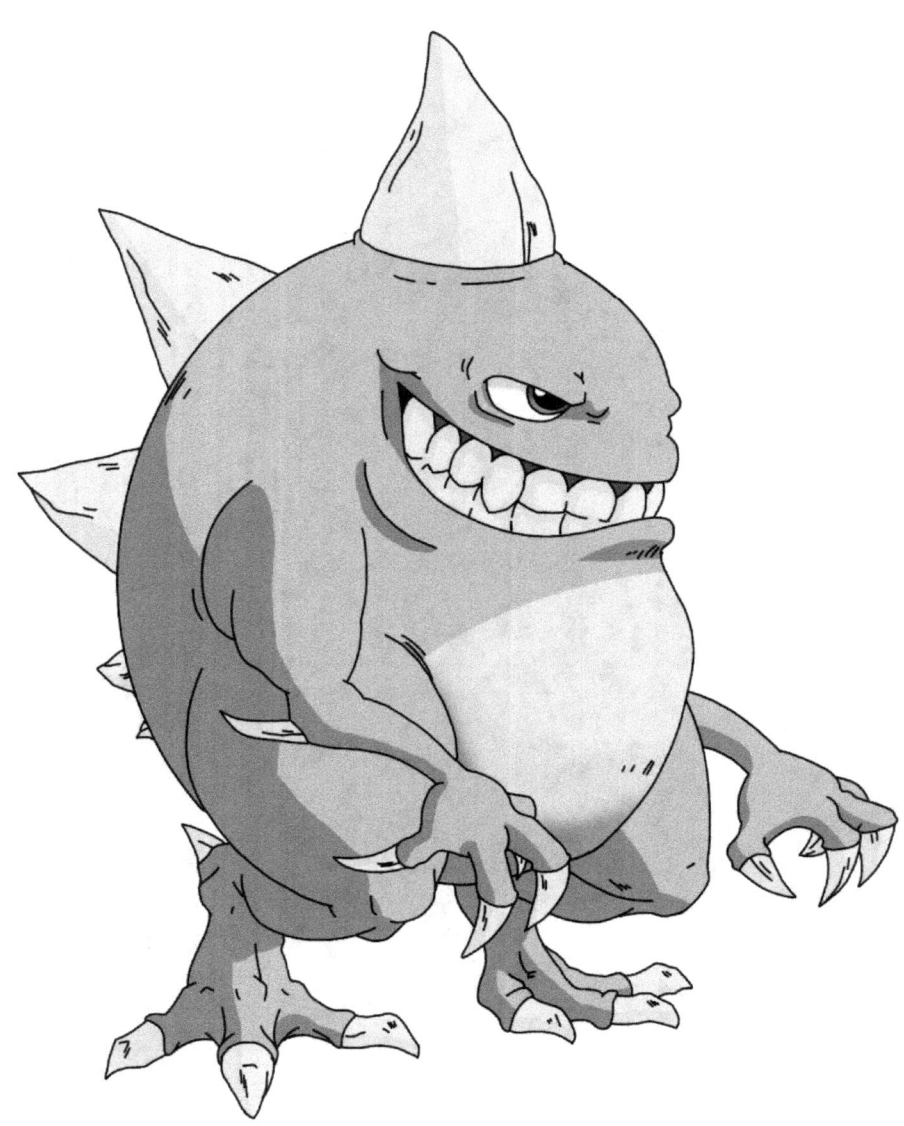

Add some shadow to give him more volume.

Step 16.

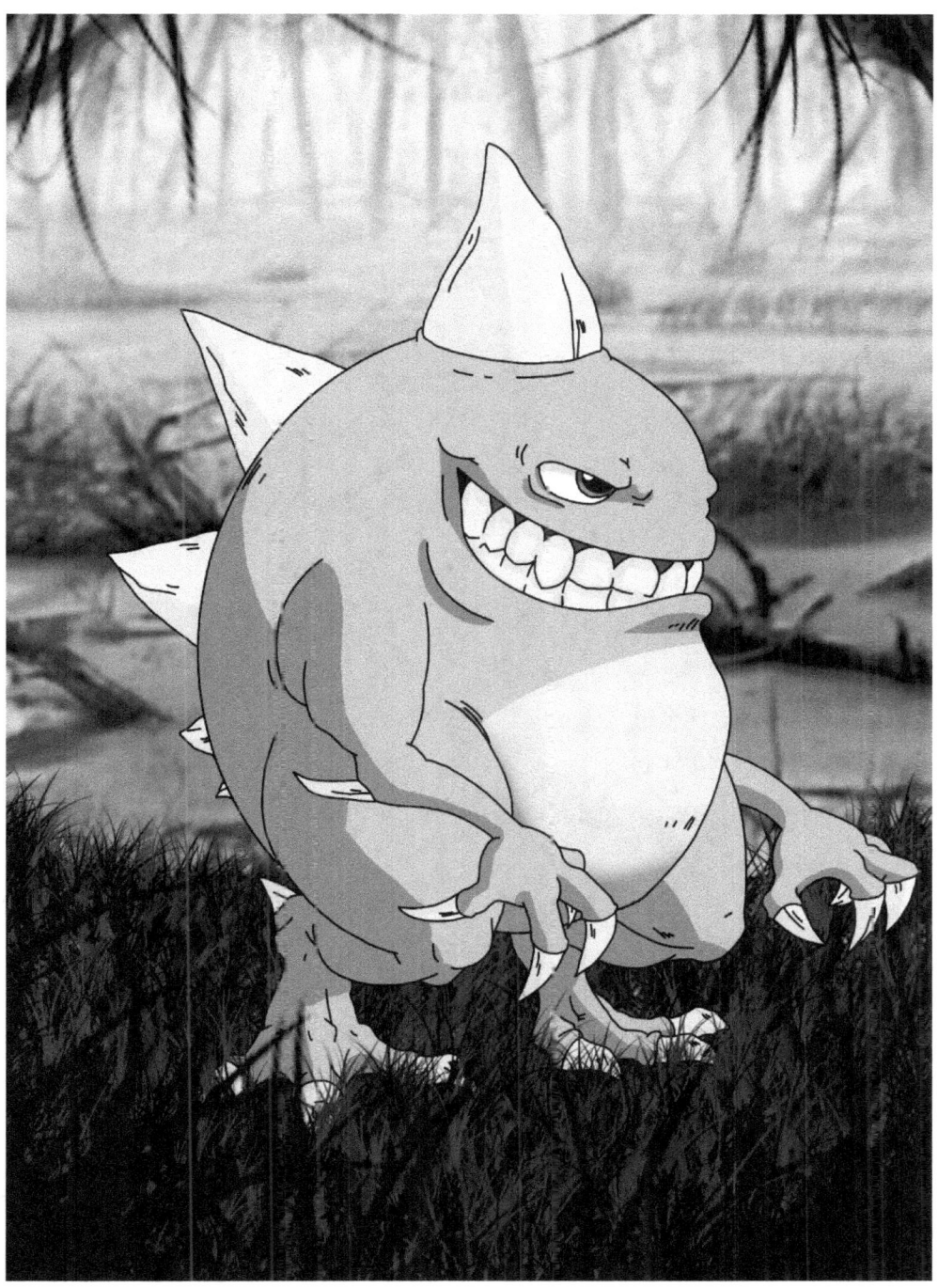

Colored version.

Step 17.

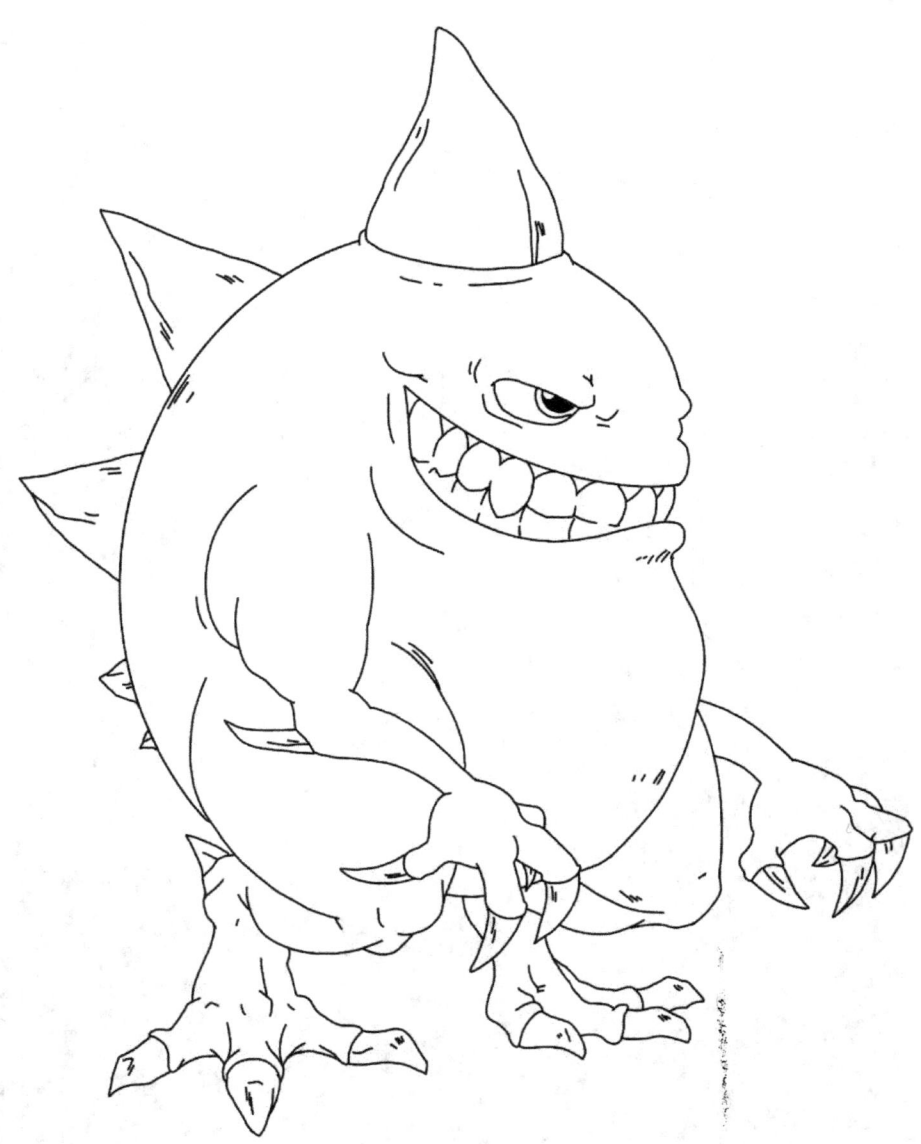

Line art version.

How to Draw a Green Frog

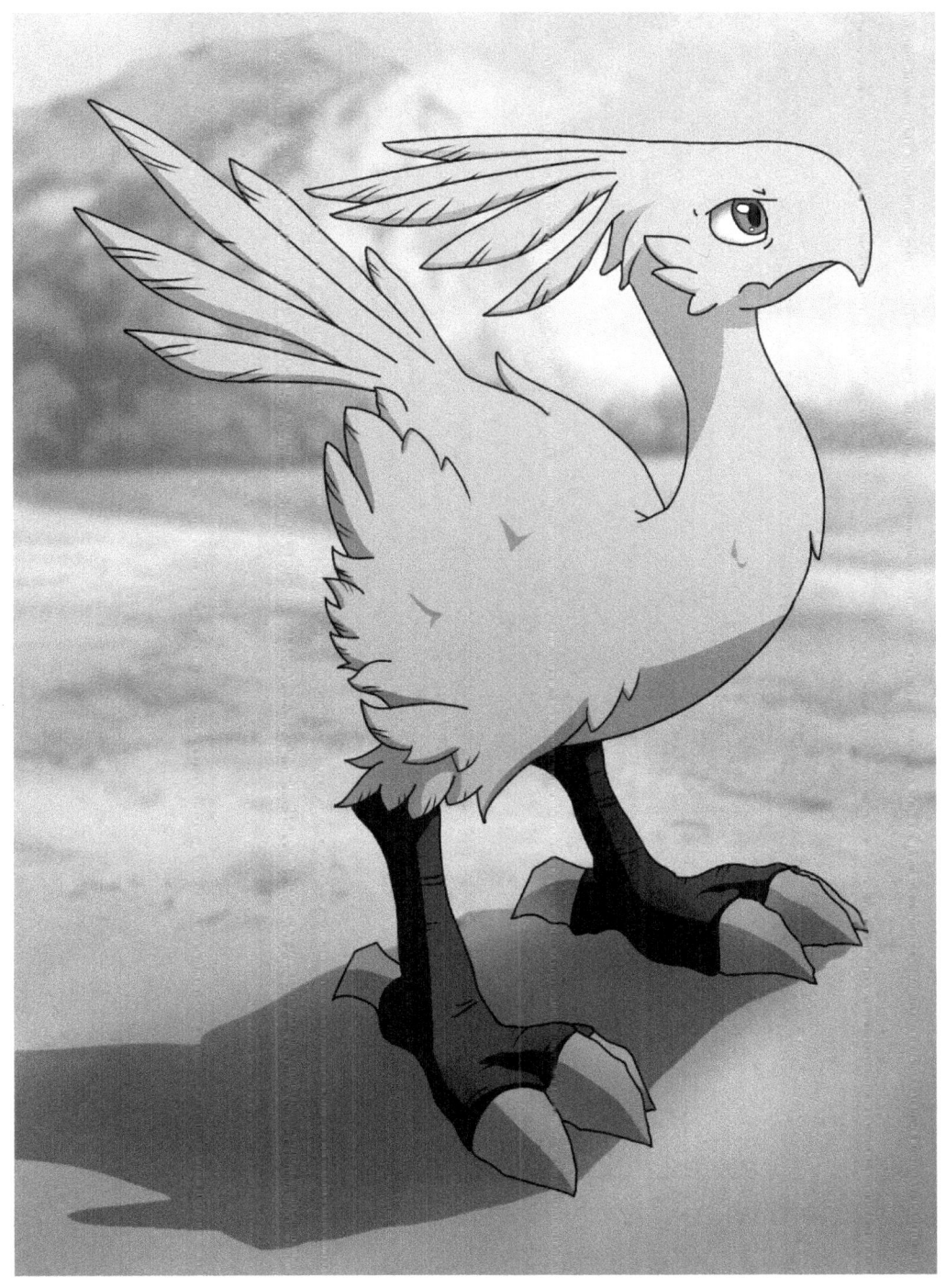

Step 1.

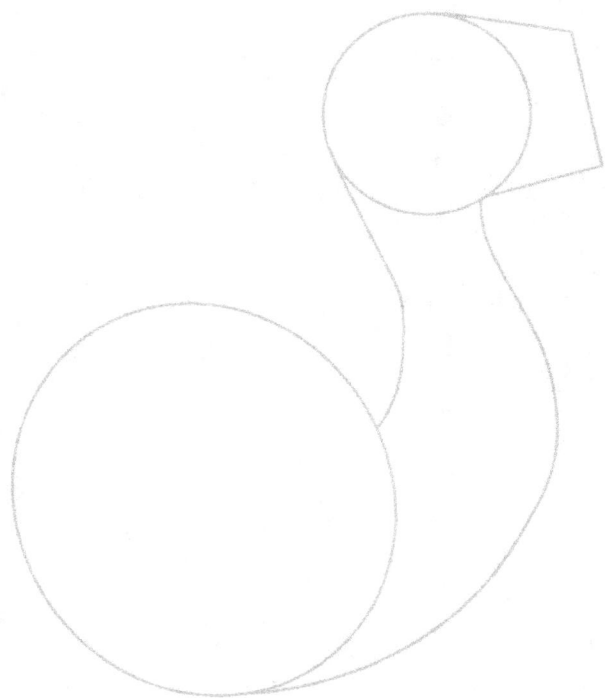

Draw a circle for the head and the body.
Connect them with a swirly neck and add the outline of the beak.

Step 2.

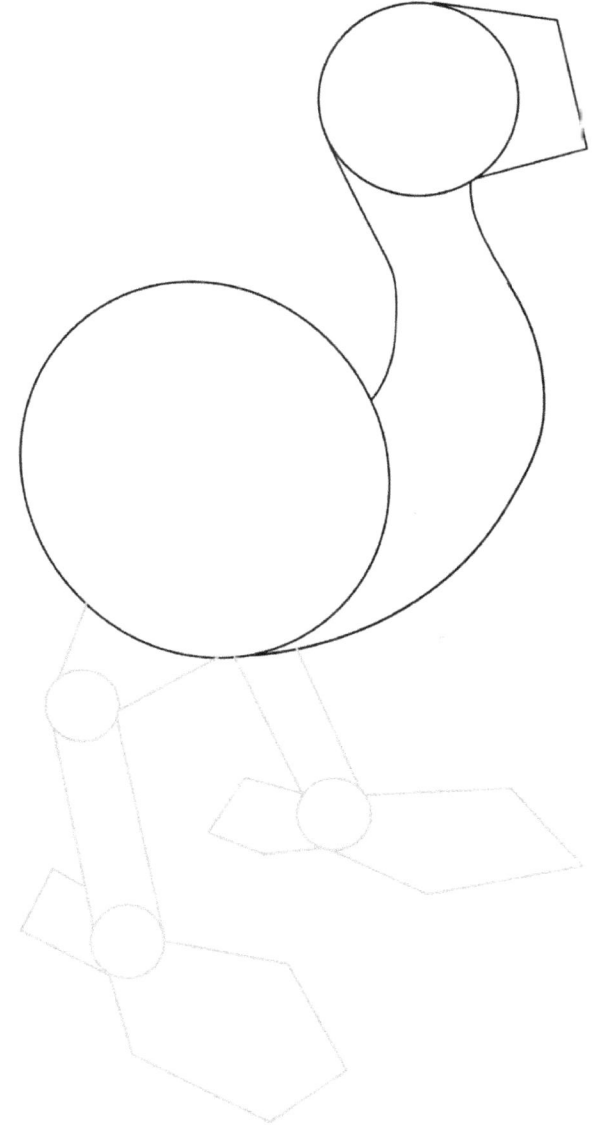

Add circles for the knees and ankles.
Connect them to make the legs and add the outline of the feet.

Step 3.

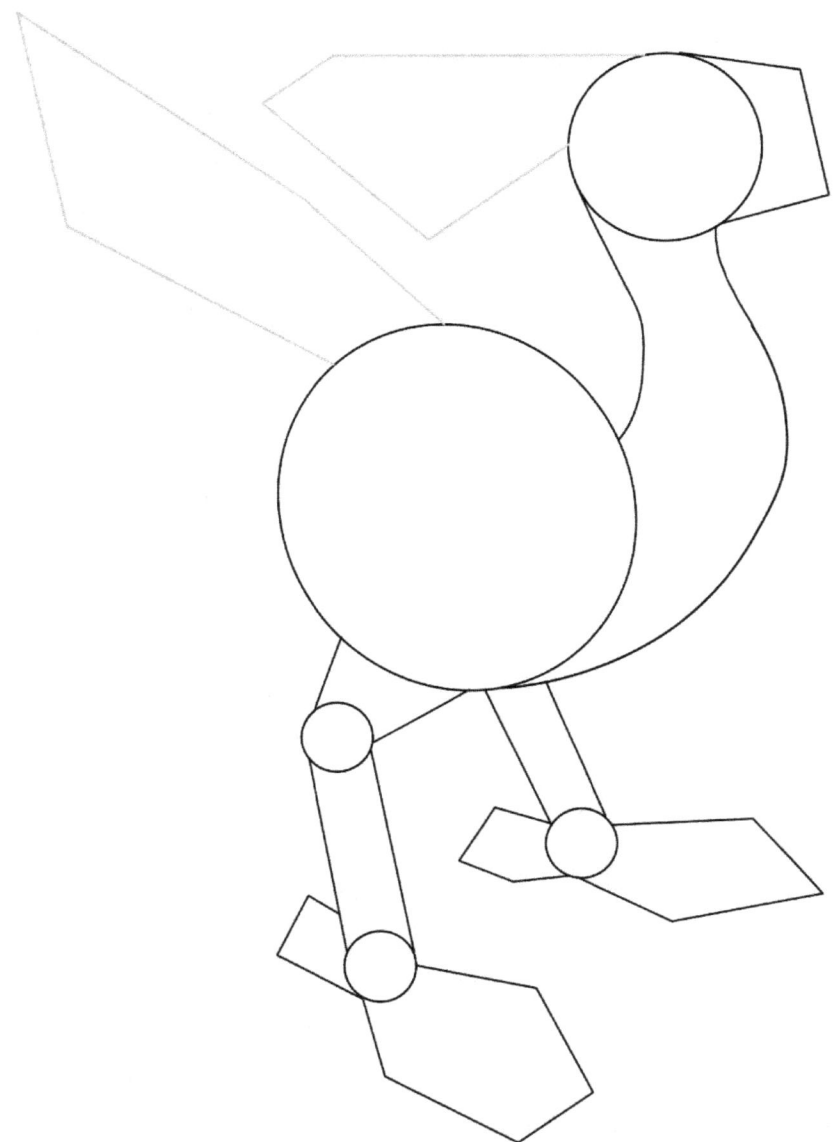

Add the outline of the tail feathers and the head feathers.

Step 4.

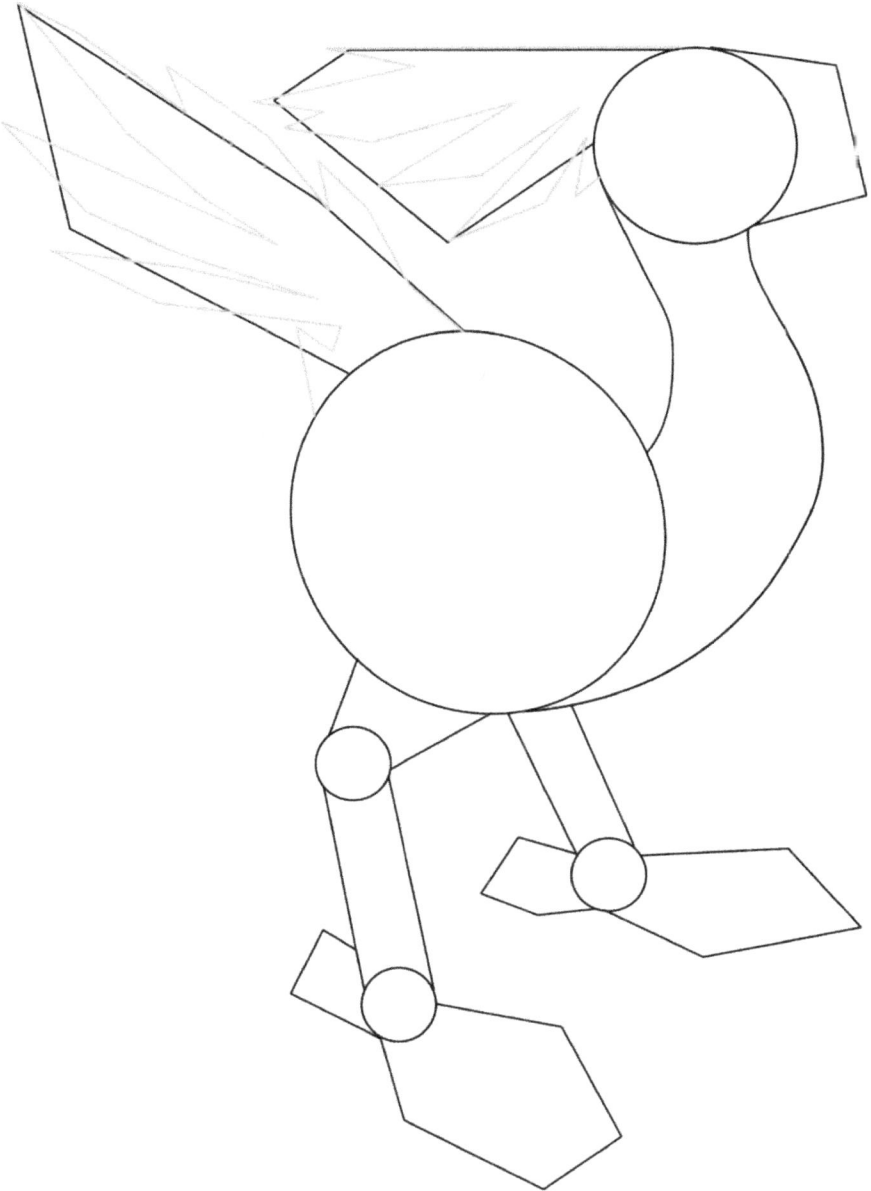

Redraw them to make some cool spikey looking feathers. Don't worry, we will finish these later, but first we focus on the big shapes.

Step 5.

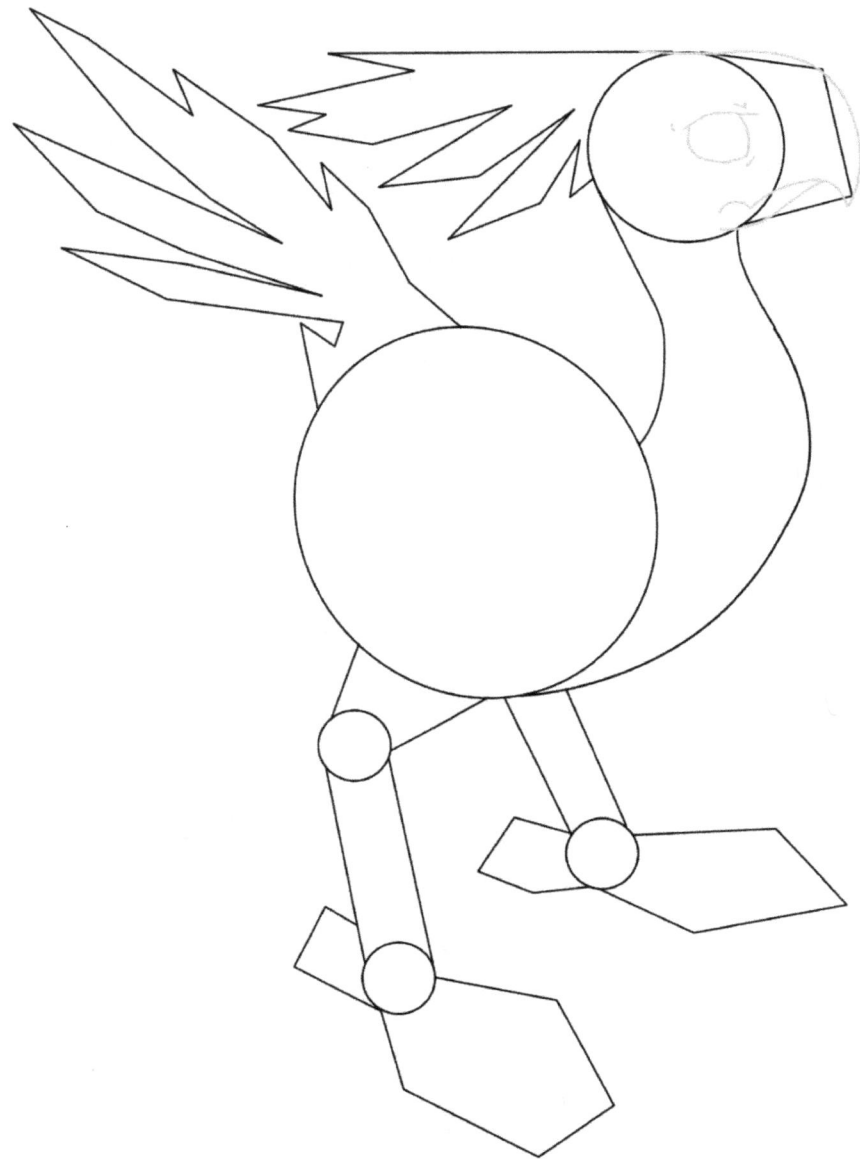

Redraw the beak and reshape the head.
Make the beak pointy and add a slightly disappointed smile.
Then add a big eye to the head.

Step 6.

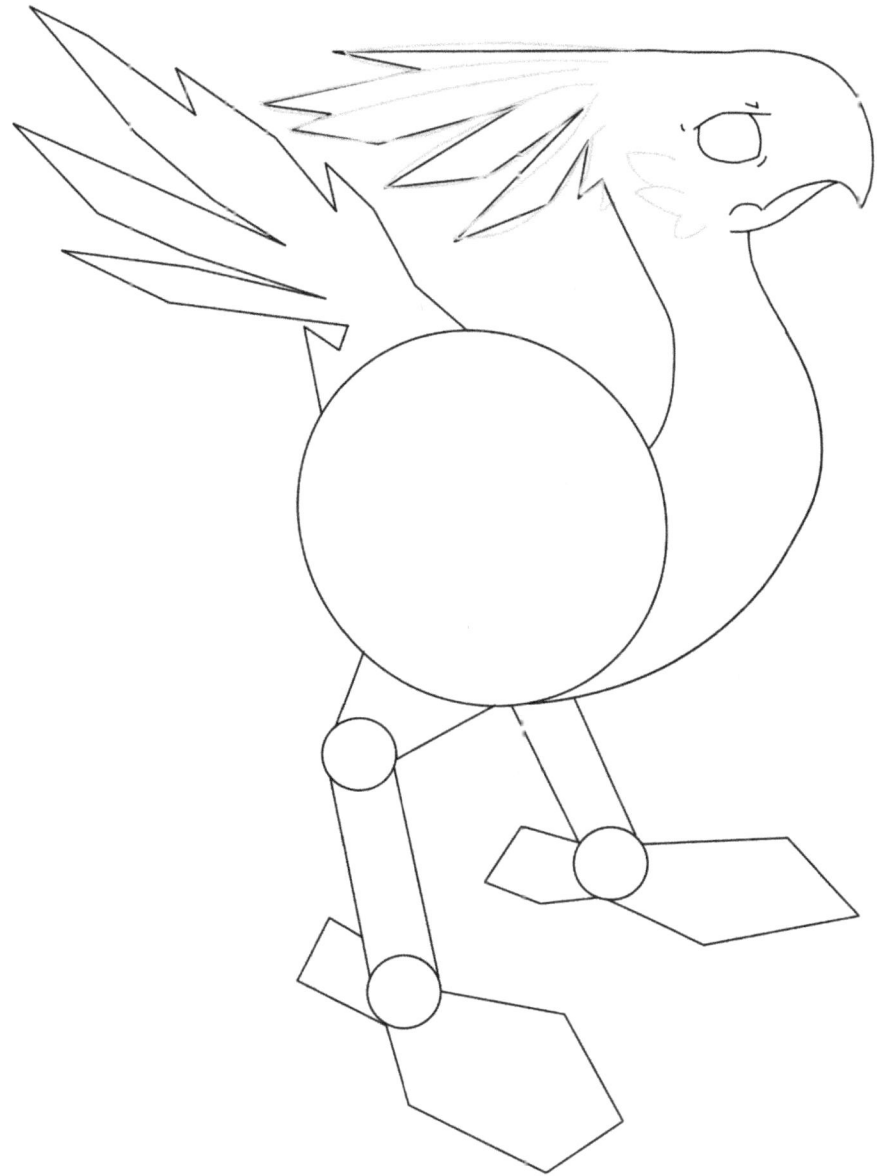

Redraw the head feathers to make them smoother and softer looking.
Then add a few feathers for the cheek

Step 7.

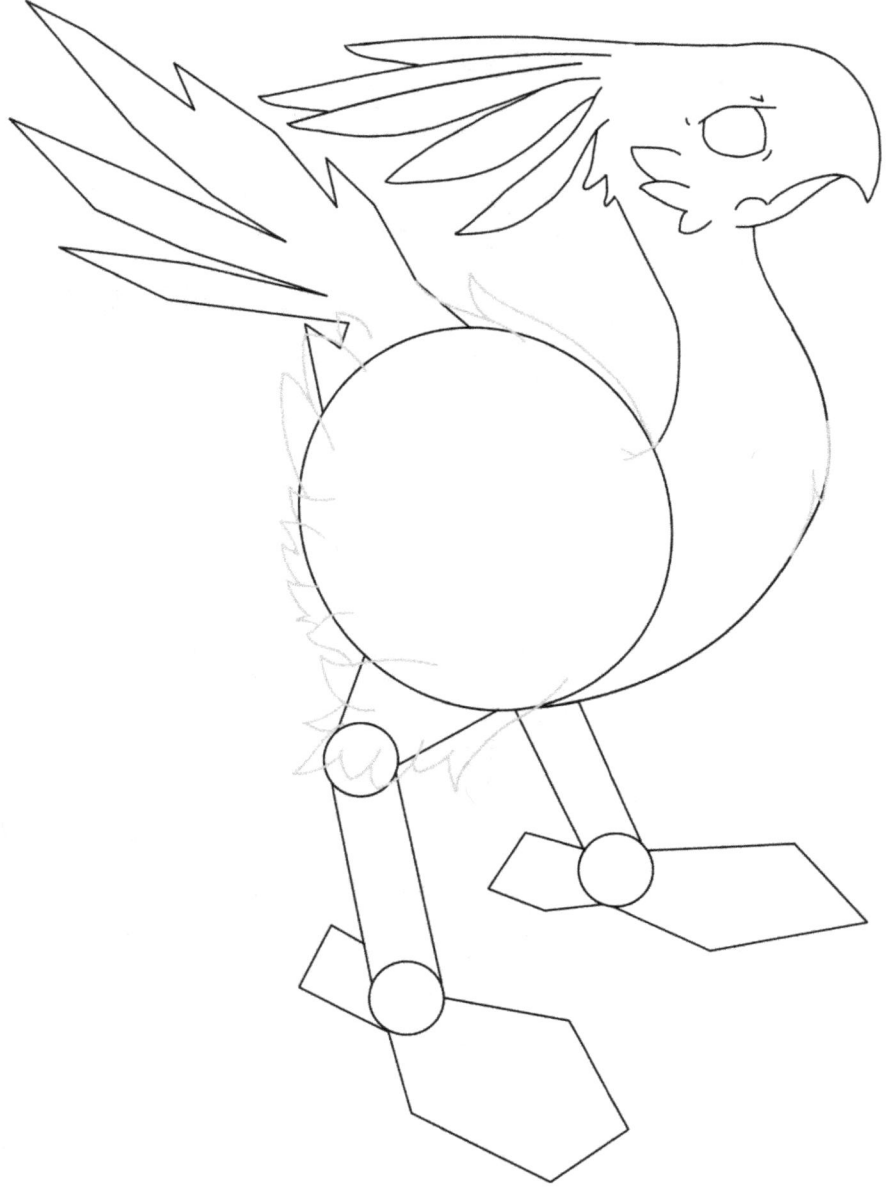

Redraw his body to give it more volume.
Use the example to show how the feathers are drawn around the legs and the back of the body.

Step 8.

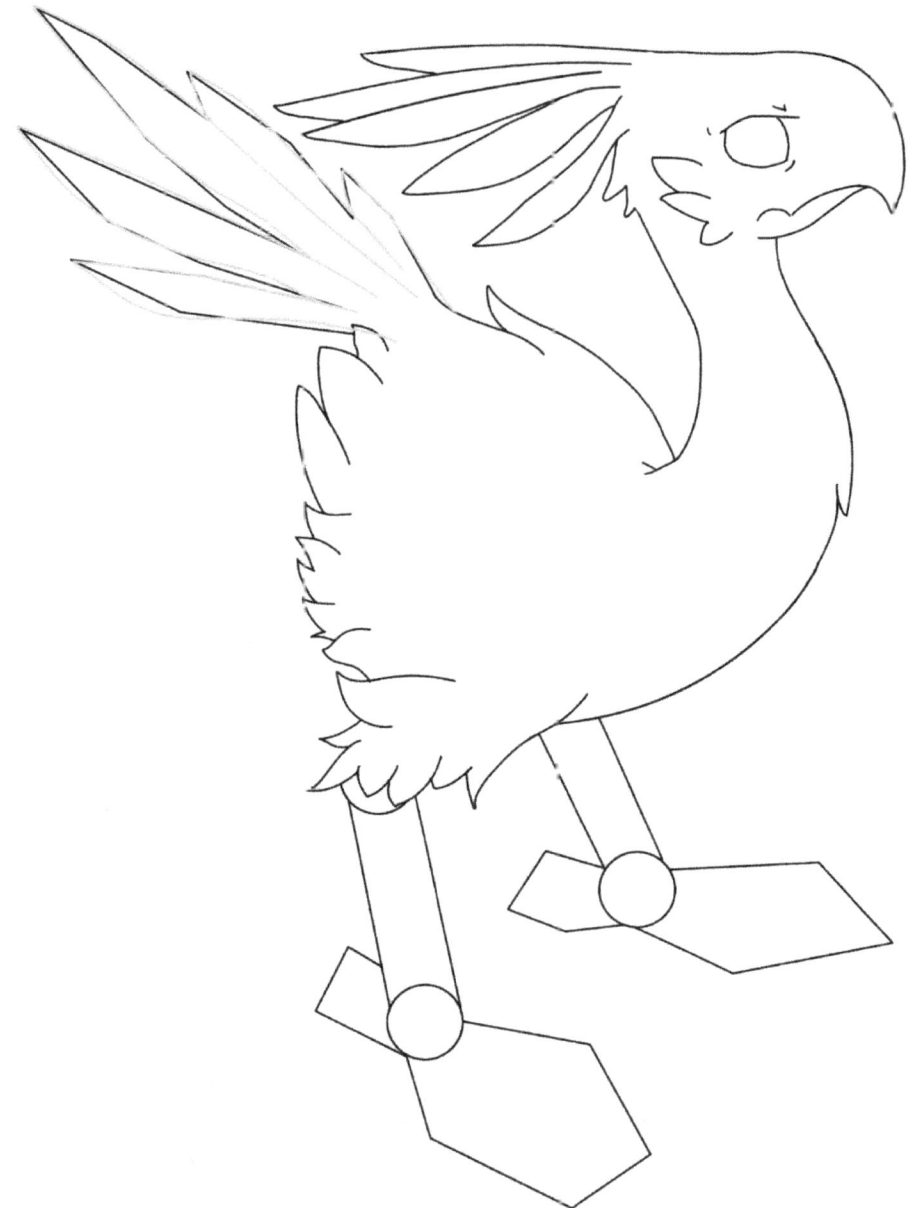

Now redraw the tail fathers to make them smoother and softer looking.

Step 9.

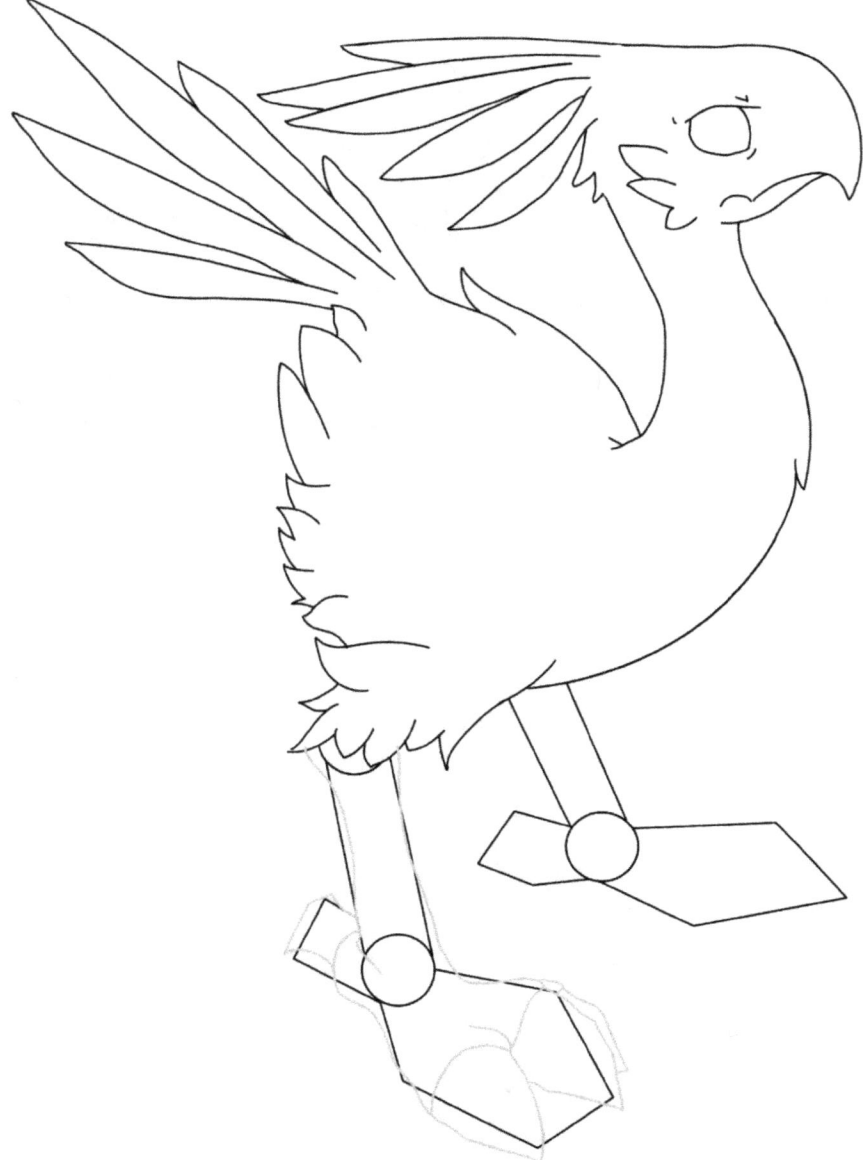

Continue with the right leg.
See how the feet had 4 toes; three in the front and one on the back.
Give them a big sharp nail.

Step 10.

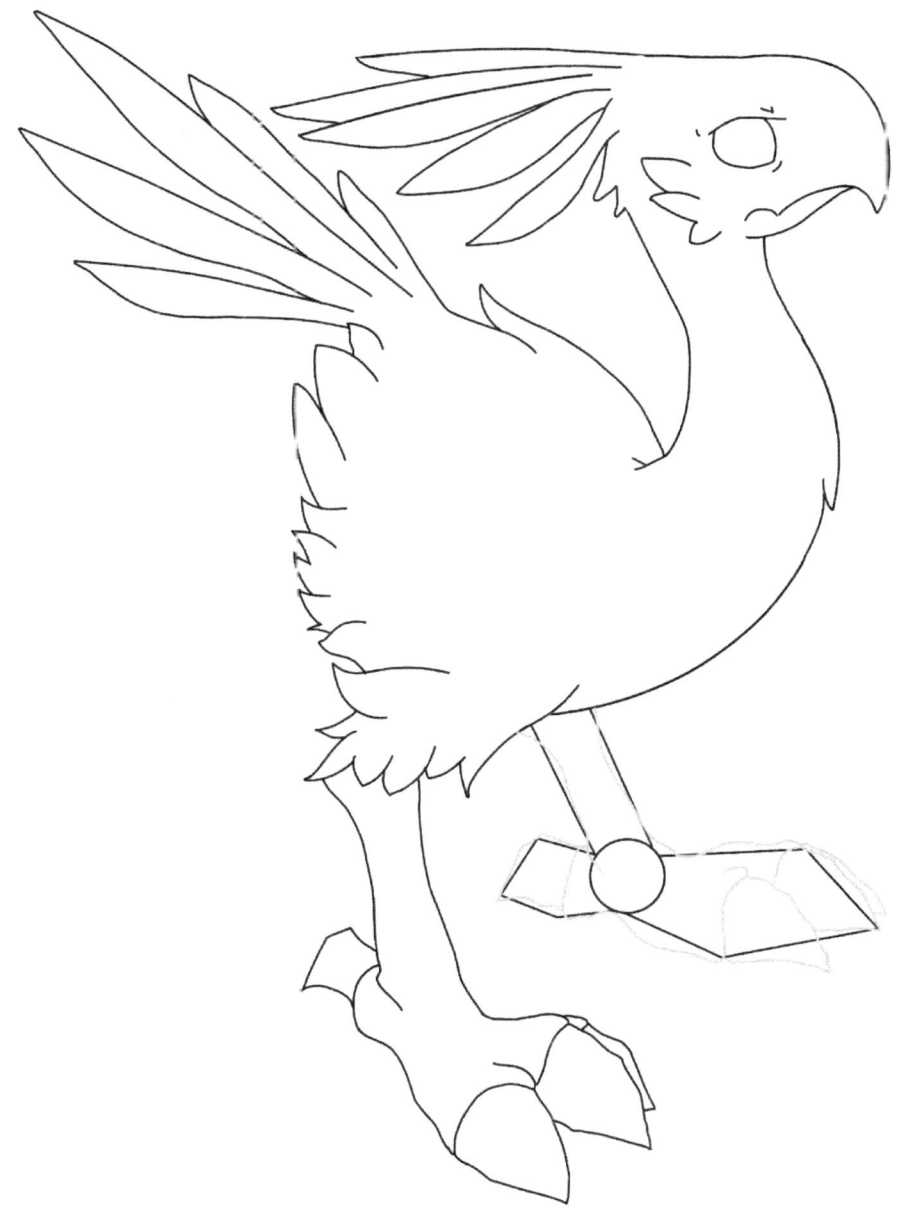

Do the same for the left foot.

Step 11.

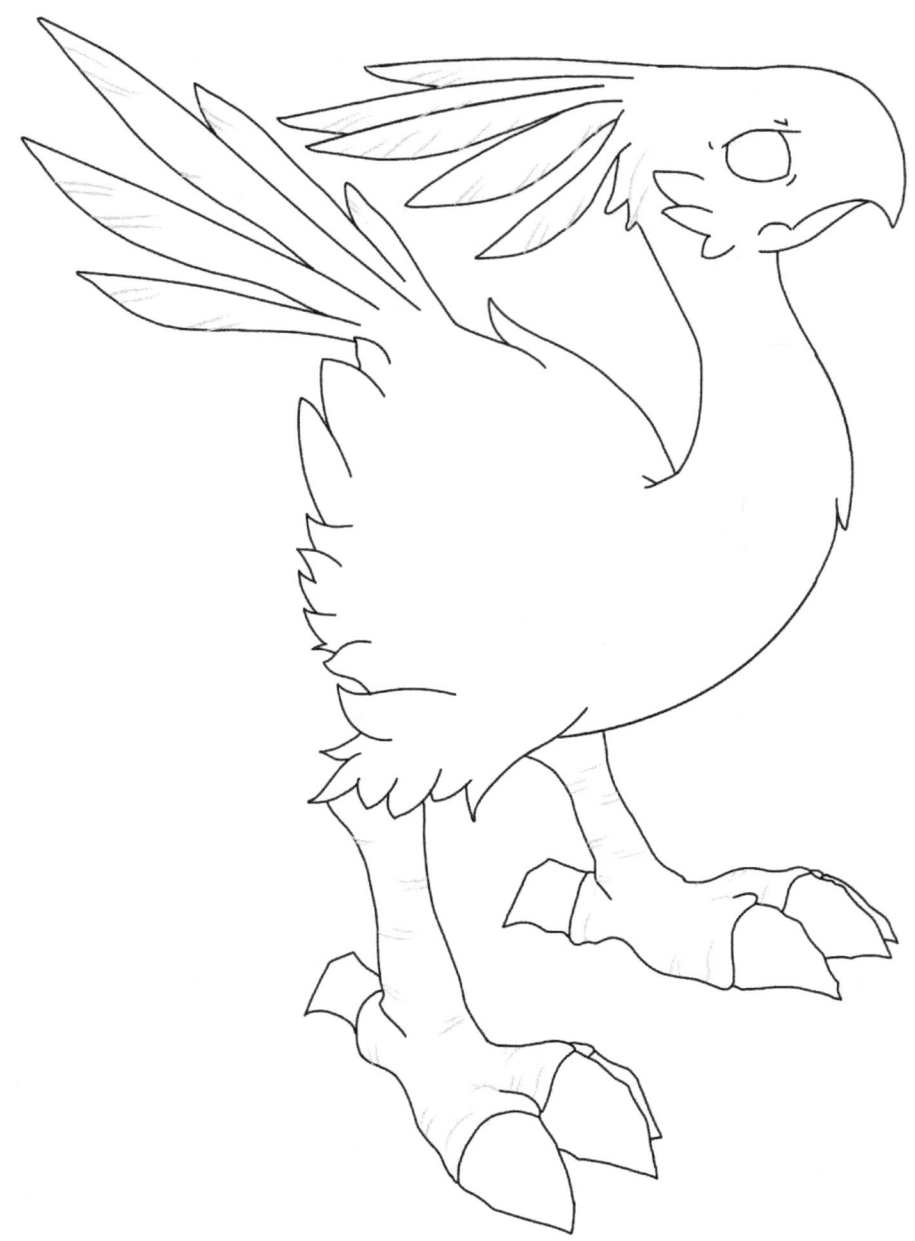

Now we'll do some detailing.
Give the feathers a few lines pointing inwards to give them more of a feathery look.

Then add lines to the legs to show that the skin on them is tough.

Step 12.

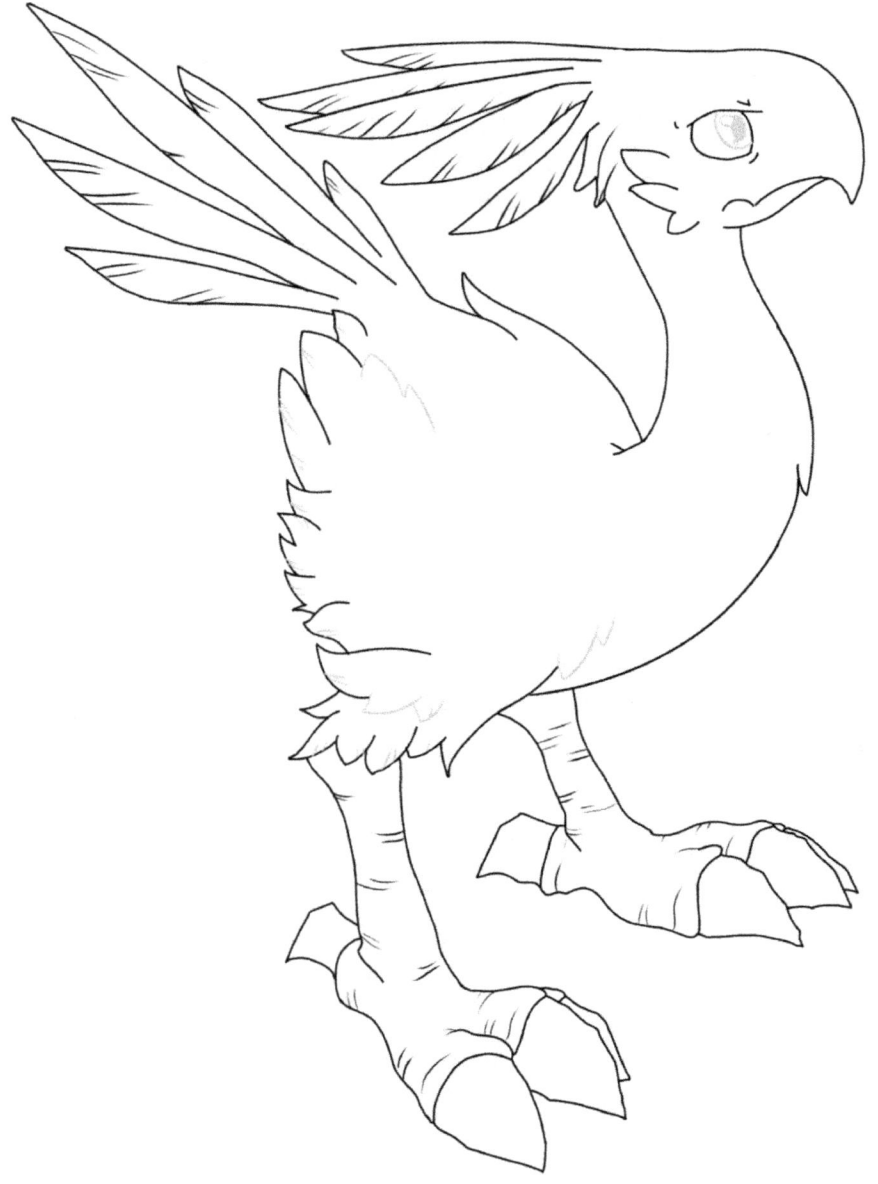

Add a big pupil to the eye.
Add some more feather shapes inside the body and some lines for detail.

Step 13.

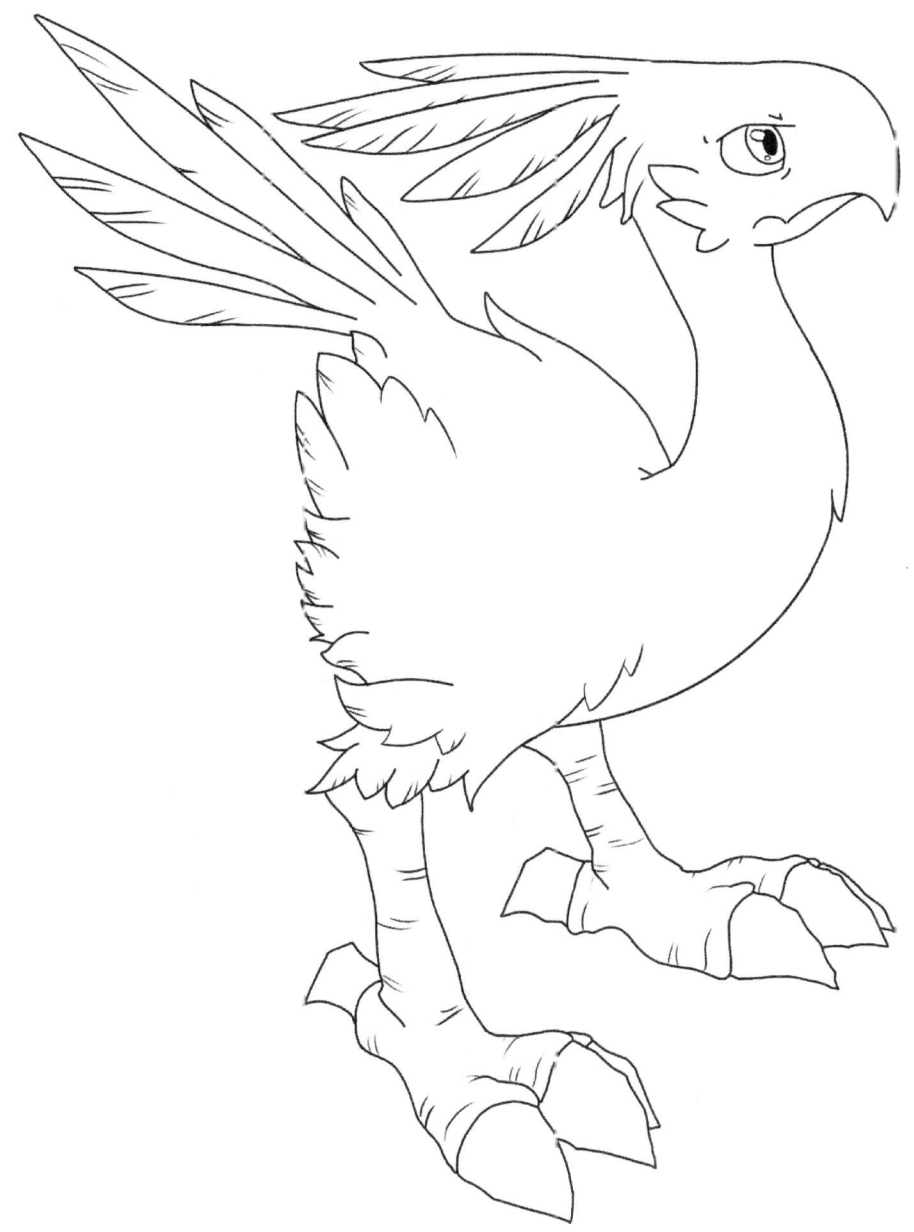

All done! Let's color!

Step 14.

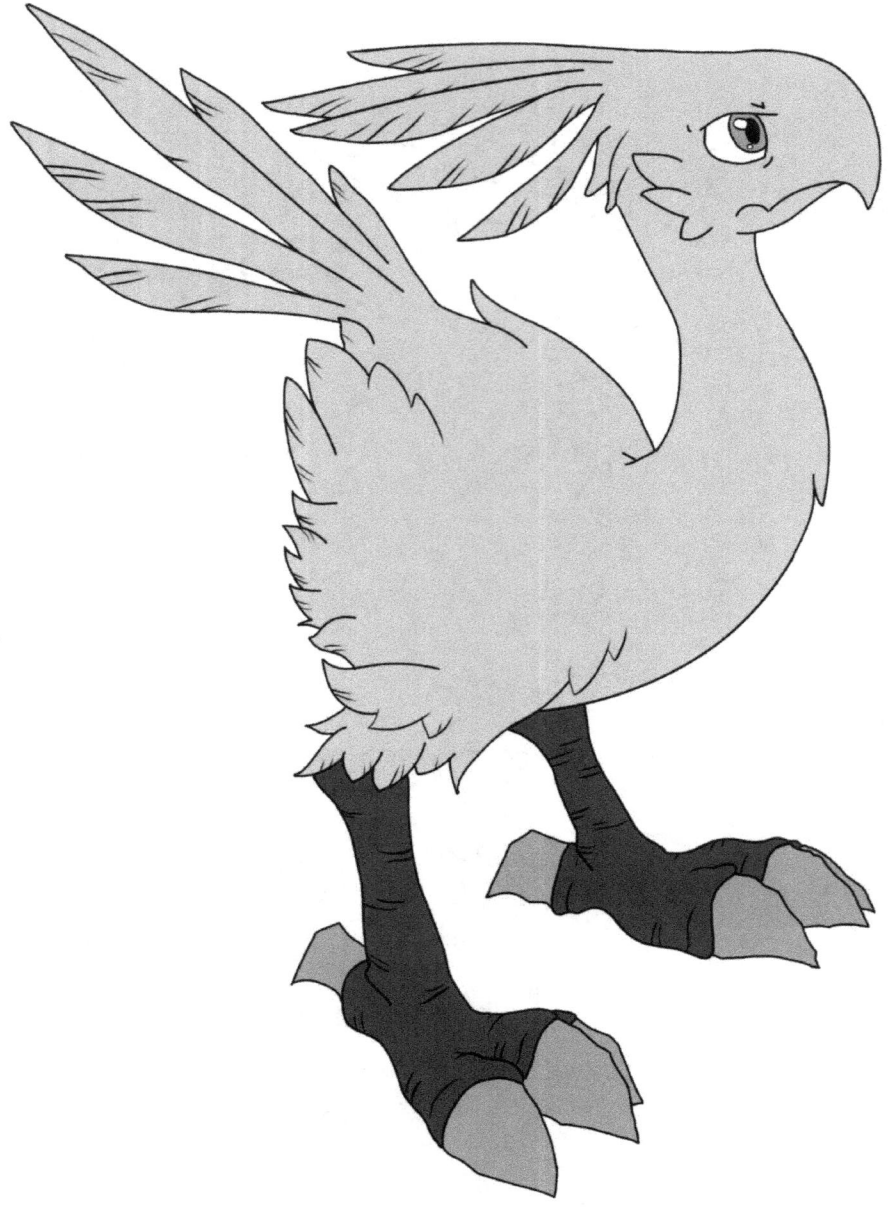

His body is yellow and his eye is red.
The legs are a dark brown and the nails are grey.

Step 15.

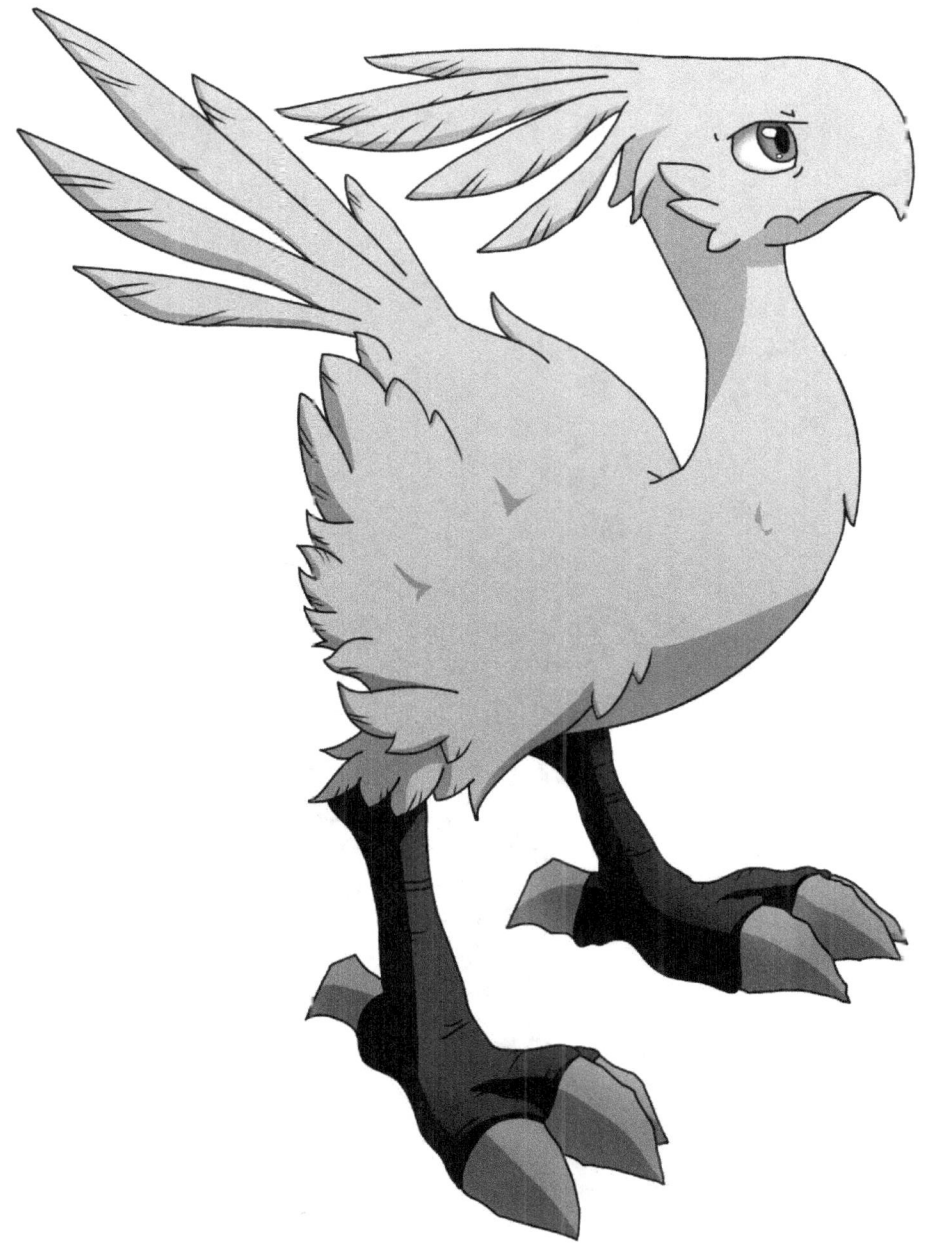

Add some shadow to give him more volume.

Step 16.

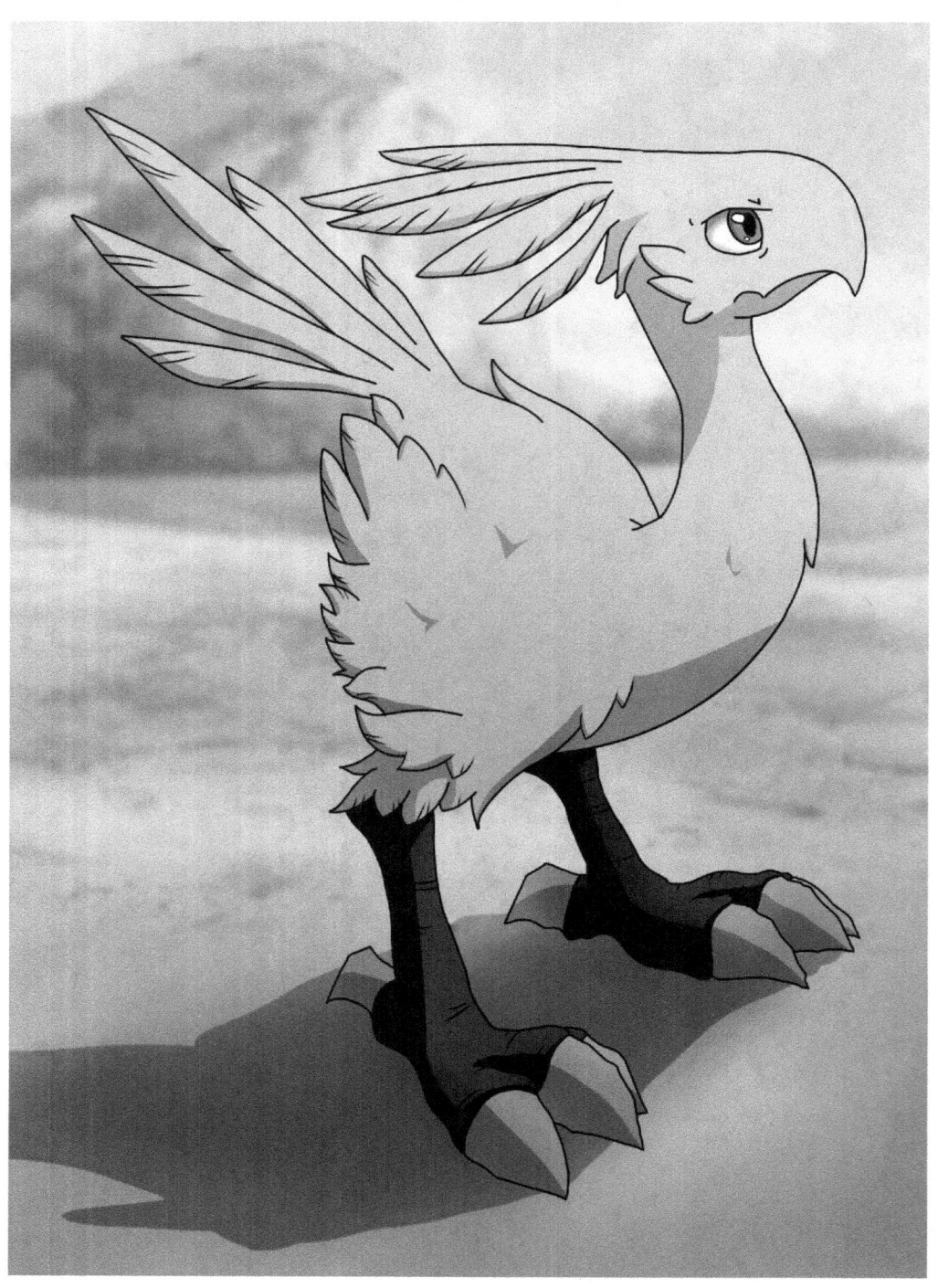

Colored version.

Step 17.

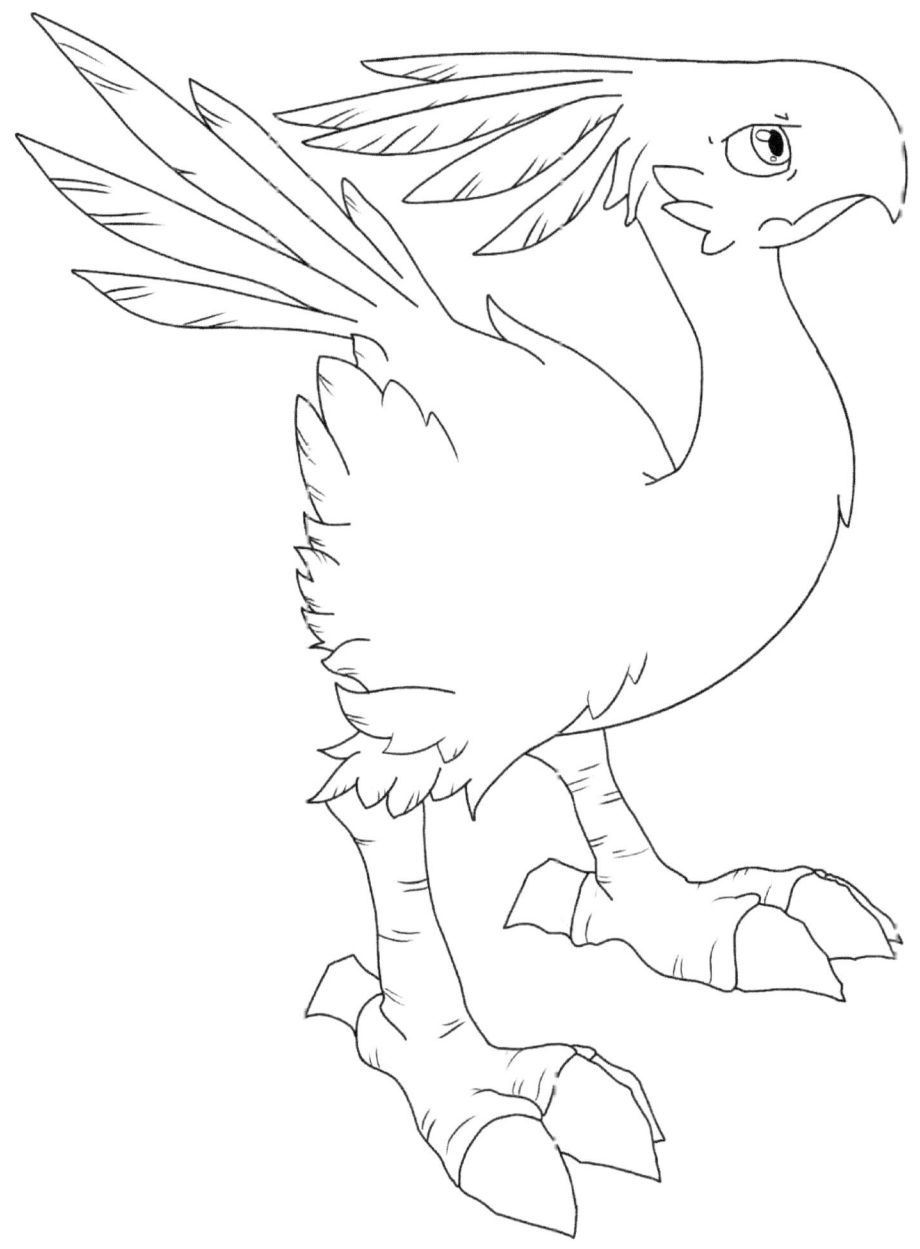

Line art version.